THE **5 *love*** LANGUAGES®

OF CHILDREN

THE 5 love LANGUAGES® OF CHILDREN

The Secret to Loving Children Effectively

Gary Chapman
Ross Campbell

NORTHFIELD PUBLISHING

CHICAGO

Scripture quotations marked NIV are taken from the *Holy Bible, New International Version*®, NIV®. © 1973, 1978, 1984, 2011 by Biblica, Inc.™ Used by permission of Zondervan. All rights reserved worldwide. www.zondervan.com. The "NIV" and "New International Version" are trademarks registered in the United States Patent and Trademark Office by Biblica, Inc.™

Scripture quotations marked NKJV are taken from the *New King James Version.* © 1979, 1980, 1982 by Thomas Nelson, Inc. Used by permission. All rights reserved.

Edited by Elizabeth Cody Newenhuyse
Cover design: Faceout Studios
Cover photo: Boone Rodriguez (boonerodriguez.com)
Interior design: Smartt Guys design

Library of Congress Cataloging-in-Publication Data

Names: Chapman, Gary D., 1938- author. | Campbell, Ross, 1936- author. |
  Campbell, Ross.
Title: The 5 love languages of children : the secret to loving children
  effectively / Gary D Chapman, Ross Campbell.
Other titles: Five love languages of children
Description: Chicago : Northfield Publishing, 2016. | Includes
  bibliographical references.
Identifiers: LCCN 2016010089 (print) | LCCN 2016015614 (ebook) | ISBN
  9780802412850 (paperback) | ISBN 9780802493767 ()
Subjects: LCSH: Interpersonal communication in children. | Parent and child.
  | Child psychology. | BISAC: FAMILY & RELATIONSHIPS / Parenting / General.
  | FAMILY & RELATIONSHIPS / Life Stages / School Age. | EDUCATION /
  Elementary.
Classification: LCC BF723.C57 C47 2016 (print) | LCC BF723.C57 (ebook) | DDC
  649/.1--dc23
LC record available at https://lccn.loc.gov/2016010089

We hope you enjoy this book from Northfield Publishing. Our goal is to provide high-quality, thought-provoking books and products that connect truth to your real needs and challenges. For more information on other books and products that will help you with all your important relationships, go to 5lovelanguages.com or write to:

Northfield Publishing
820 N. LaSalle Blvd.
Chicago, IL 60610

7 9 10 8 6

Printed in the United States of America

Contents

THE 5 love LANGUAGES® OF CHILDREN

Speaking Your Child's Love Language

D oes your child feel loved?

"Of course," you say. "I tell her every day." But are you communicating that love in a way she understands?

Every child has a primary language of love, a way in which he or she understands a parent's love best. This book will show you how to recognize and speak your child's primary love language as well as the four other love languages that can help your child know you love him or her. As we will see, your child needs to *know* he is loved in order to grow into a giving, loving, responsible adult.

The 5 Love Languages of Children will introduce you to all five love languages of children and help you determine the primary languages in which your child hears your love. Be careful to read all five chapters (2–6) that describe the love languages, as your child will benefit from all five ways of receiving love. Practice all five love languages and you can be sure your child will sense your love. To help you do this, each chapter ends with practical ideas for helping you speak that love language with your children.

But how can you know what your child's love language is? Turn to chapter 7 for ideas.

All aspects of a child's development require a foundation of love. As a book about learning to better love your child, *The 5 Love Languages of Children* includes suggestions throughout for good parenting. As you work on those areas that are most important, you will find that your family relationships will be stronger and also more relaxed and enjoyable.

And now, a personal word from Gary as you begin this "language course" to improve the way you speak love to your children.

A Word from Gary

The success of *The 5 Love Languages: The Secret to Love That Lasts* has been gratifying. Millions of couples have not only read the book, but have practiced its principles. My files are filled with letters from couples all over the world, expressing gratitude for the difference the love languages have made in their marriages. Most tell me that learning the primary love language of their spouse has made a radical change in the emotional climate of their home, and some have credited the book with actually saving their marriage.

This book grew out of the many requests I received to "write a book on the five love languages of children." Because my professional career has focused on marriage counseling and enrichment, I was reluctant at first to write about children, even though I received hundreds of reports from parents who applied the concept of the love languages to their children.

When Northfield Publishing talked with me about doing such a book, I contacted my friend of many years, Ross Campbell, to ask him to coauthor the book with me. Dr. Campbell spent many years in psychiatric medicine, with a focus on the needs of children and adolescents. His contributions proved invaluable.

Just as the original book on love languages has helped so many people in their marriages, so now I hope that this book will aid countless parents, teachers, and others who love and work with children to become more effective in meeting the emotional need children have for love.

GARY CHAPMAN, PHD
Winston-Salem, North Carolina

THE 5 love LANGUAGES

OF CHILDREN

1

Love Is the Foundation

B rad and Emily couldn't figure out what was wrong with Caleb, their eight-year-old son. He had been an above-average learner and still did his homework, but this year he was struggling in school. He would go to the teacher after she had given an exercise and ask her to explain it again. He'd visit her desk up to eight times a day, asking for further instructions. Was it poor hearing or a comprehension problem? Brad and Emily had Caleb's hearing tested, and a school counselor gave him a comprehension test. His hearing was normal and his understanding typical for a third-grader.

Other things about their son puzzled them. At times, Caleb's behavior seemed almost antisocial. The teacher would take turns eating with her third-grade students during lunch, but Caleb would sometimes push other children aside so he could be near her. During recess, he would leave other children whenever the teacher appeared on the playground, running to her to ask an insignificant question and escape the others. If the teacher participated in a game during recess, Caleb would try to hold the teacher's hand during the game.

His parents had met with the teacher three times already, and neither they nor the teacher could find the problem. Independent and happy in grades one and two, Caleb now seemed to show "clinging behavior" that made no sense. He also was fighting much more with his older sister, Hannah, although Emily and Brad assumed that was just a stage he was passing through.

When this couple came to my "The Marriage You've Always Wanted" seminar and told me about Caleb, they were worried, wondering if they had a budding rebel on their hands, or maybe a kid with psychological problems. "Dr. Chapman, we know this is a marriage seminar and maybe our question is out of place," Emily said, "but Brad and I thought that perhaps you could give us some guidance." Then she described her son's worrisome behavior.

I asked these parents whether their own lifestyle had changed this year. Brad said he was a salesman, out on calls two nights a week, but home between 6:00 and 7:30 p.m. on the other weeknights. Those nights were spent catching up on emails and texts and watching a little TV. On weekends, he used to go to football games, often taking Caleb. But he hadn't done that in a year. "It's just too much of a hassle. I'd rather watch the games on TV."

"How about you, Emily?" I asked. "Have there been any changes in your lifestyle over the last few months?"

"Definitely," she said. "I've been working part-time at the college for the last three years since Caleb entered kindergarten. But this year I took a full-time job there, so I get home later than usual. Actually my mom picks him up at school, and Caleb stays with her for about an hour and a half until I pick him up. On the evenings that Brad is out of town, Caleb and I usually have dinner with my folks and then come home."

It was almost time for the seminar session to begin, yet I sensed I was beginning to understand what was going on inside of Caleb. So I made a suggestion. "I'm going to be talking about marriage, but I want each of you to be thinking about how the principles I am sharing might apply to your relationship with Caleb. At the end of the seminar, I'd like to know what conclusions you have drawn." They seemed a little surprised that I was ending our conversation without making any suggestions, but they both were willing to go along with my request.

At the end of the day, as other participants at our seminar were filing out, Brad and Emily hurried up to me with that look of fresh discovery. "Dr. Chapman, I think we have just gained some insight into what's going on with Caleb," Emily said. "When you were discussing the five love languages, we both agreed that Caleb's primary love language is *quality time*. Looking back over the last four or five months, we realized that we have given him less quality time than we had before.

"When I was working part-time, I'd pick him up from school every day, and we would usually do something together on the way home, maybe run an errand or stop by the park or get ice cream together. When we got home, Caleb would play games on his tablet for a while. Then after dinner, I would often help him with his homework or we'd watch something on Netflix, especially on the nights Brad was away. All that has changed since I started my new job, and I realize I'm spending less time with Caleb."

I glanced at Brad, and he said, "For my part, I realize I used to take Caleb with me to football games, but since I stopped going, I haven't replaced that father-son time with anything. He and I haven't really spent a great deal of time together the last few months. I need to think about ways I can 'check in' with him when I'm traveling, too."

"I think you may have discovered some real insight into Caleb's emotional need," I told them. "If you can meet his need for love, I think there is a good chance you will see a change in his behavior." I suggested some key ways to express love through quality time and challenged Brad to build time with Caleb into his schedule, even "long-distance" time. I encouraged Emily to look for ways she and Caleb could once more do some of the things they did before she started her full-time job. They both seemed eager to translate their insight into action.

"There may be other factors involved," I said, "but if you will give your son large doses of quality time and then sprinkle in the other four love languages, I think you will see a radical change in his behavior."

We said goodbye. I never heard from Emily and Brad, and to be honest, I forgot about them. But about two years later I returned to Wisconsin for another seminar, and they walked in and reminded me of our conversation. They were all smiles; we hugged each other, and they introduced me to friends they had invited to the seminar.

"Tell me about Caleb," I said.

They both smiled and said, "He's doing great. We meant to write you many times but never got around to it. We went home and did what you suggested. We consciously gave Caleb lots of quality time over the next few months. Within two or three weeks, really, we saw a dramatic change in his behavior at school. In fact, the teacher asked us to come in again, and we were worried. But this time, she wanted to ask what we had done that had brought about such a change in Caleb."

The teacher told them that Caleb's inappropriate behavior had stopped: no more pushing other children away from her in the lunch-room; no more coming to her desk to ask question after question.

Then Emily explained that her husband and she had begun to speak Caleb's "love language" after attending a seminar. "We told her how we had started giving him overdoses of quality time," said Emily.

This couple had learned to speak their son's love language, to say, "I love you" in a way that Caleb could understand. His story encouraged me to write this book.

Speaking your child's primary love language does not mean he or she will not rebel later. It does mean your child will know you love him, and that can bring him security and hope; it can help you to rear your child to responsible adulthood. Love is the foundation.

In raising children, everything depends on the love relationship between the parent and child. Nothing works well if a child's love needs are not met. Only the child who *feels* genuinely loved and cared for can do her best. You may truly love your child, but unless she feels it—unless you speak the love language that communicates to her your love—she will not feel loved.

FILLING THE EMOTIONAL TANK

By speaking your child's own love language, you can fill his "emotional tank" with love. When your child feels loved, he is much easier to discipline and train than when his "emotional tank" is running near empty.

Every child has an emotional tank, a place of emotional strength that can fuel him through the challenging days of childhood and adolescence. Just as cars are powered by reserves in the gas tank, our children are fueled from their emotional tanks. We must fill our children's emotional tanks for them to operate as they should and reach their potential.

But with what do we fill these tanks? Love, of course, but love of a particular kind that will enable our children to grow and function properly.

We need to fill our children's emotional tanks with unconditional love, because real love is always unconditional. Unconditional love is a full love that accepts and affirms a child for who he is, not for what he does. No matter what he does (or does not do), the parent still loves him. Sadly, some parents display a love that is conditional; it depends on something other than their children just being. Conditional love is based on performance and is often associated with training techniques that offer gifts, rewards, and privileges to children who behave or perform in desired ways.

Of course, it is necessary to train and discipline our children—but only after their emotional tanks have been filled (and refilled—they can deplete regularly). Only unconditional love can prevent problems such as resentment, feelings of being unloved, guilt, fear, and insecurity. Only as we give our children unconditional love will we be able to deeply understand them and deal with their behaviors, whether good or bad.

Ana remembers growing up in a home of modest financial resources. Her father was employed at a plant nearby and her mother was a homemaker, except for occasionally working at Target. Both parents were hardworking people who took pride in their house and family. Ana helped her mom cook the evening meal, and later she, her dad, and brothers would pitch in on cleanup and then watch some TV. Saturday was a day for weekly chores and the occasional youth soccer game, and Saturday nights they sent out for pizza. On Sunday mornings, the family went to church and that evening they would spend time with relatives.

When Ana and her brothers were younger, their parents would

listen to them practice their reading almost every night. They always encouraged them in their studies because they wanted all three children to attend college, even though they did not have this opportunity themselves.

In middle school, Ana spent a lot of time with Sophia. The two had most classes together, often shared lunch, texted one another. But the girls didn't visit each other at home. If they had, they would have seen vast differences. Sophia's father was a successful executive who was away from home most of the time. Sophia's mother was a doctor with a busy practice. An older sister was out of college and living out of state. The family did take vacations to places like London and LA, which Sophia loved. Her mother did her best to make time for her younger daughter and understood the dangers of lavishing her with things rather than simple attention. . . .

The girls were good friends until the ninth grade, when Sophia went off to a college-prep school near her grandparents. The first year, the girls kept in touch on social media; after that, Sophia began dating and communicated less. Ana got busy with her studies and other friendships. After Sophia's family moved away, Ana never heard from her again.

If she had, she would have been sad to know that after marrying and having one child, Sophia struggled with alcoholism and the breakup of her marriage. In contrast, Ana was in grad school studying advanced biology.

What made the difference in the outcome of two childhood friends? Although there is no one answer, we can see part of the reason in what Sophia once told her therapist: "I never felt loved by my parents. I first got involved in drinking because I wanted my friends to like me." In saying this, she wasn't trying to lay blame on her parents as much as she was trying to understand herself.

Did you notice what Sophia said? It wasn't that her parents didn't love her but that she did not feel loved. Most parents love their children and also want their children to feel loved, but few know *how* to adequately convey that feeling. It is only as they learn how to love unconditionally that they will let their children know how much they are truly loved.

A WORD OF HOPE

Raising emotionally healthy children is an increasingly difficult task these days. The influence of media (including our ever-present screens), the rise in psychological issues like narcissism, the violence and hopelessness that plague some communities, the decline in the influence of the church, even simple middle-class busyness—these things challenge families daily.

It is into such reality that we speak a word of hope to parents. We want you to enjoy a loving relationship with your children. Our focus in this book is on one exceedingly important aspect of parenting—meeting your children's need for love. We have written this book to help you give your children a greater experience of the love you have for them. This will happen as you speak the love languages they understand and can respond to.

> Whatever love language your child understands best, he needs it expressed one way— unconditionally.

Every child has a special way of perceiving love. There are five ways children (indeed, all people) speak and understand emotional love. They are *physical touch, words of affirmation, quality time, gifts,* and *acts of service.* If you have several children in your family, chances are they speak

different languages, for just as children often have different person-
alities, they may hear in different love languages. Typically, two children
need to be loved in different ways.

Whatever love language your child understands best, he needs
it expressed in one way—unconditionally. Unconditional love is a
guiding light, illuminating the darkness and enabling us as parents
to know where we are and what we need to do as we raise our child.
Without this kind of love, parenting is bewildering and confusing.

We can best define unconditional love by showing what it does.
Unconditional love shows love to a child *no matter what*. We love
regardless of what the child looks like; regardless of her assets, liabili-
ties, or handicaps; regardless of what we expect her to be; and, most
difficult of all, regardless of how she acts. This does not mean that we
like all of her behavior. It does mean that we give and show love to our
child all the time, even when her behavior is poor.

Does this sound like permissiveness? It is not. Rather, it is doing
first things first. A child with a full love tank can respond to parental
guidance without resentment.

Some people fear that this may lead to "spoiling" a child, but
that is a misconception. No child can receive too much appropriate
unconditional love. A child may be "spoiled" by a lack of training or
by inappropriate love that gives or trains incorrectly. True unconditional love will never spoil a child because it is impossible for parents
to give too much of it.

If you have not loved your children in this way, you may find it
difficult at first. But as you practice unconditional love, you will find
it has a wonderful effect, as you become a more giving and loving
person in all your relationships. No one is perfect, of course, and you
cannot expect yourself to love unconditionally all of the time. But as

you move toward that goal, you will find that you are more consistent in your ability to love, no matter what.

You may find it helpful to frequently remind yourself of some rather obvious things about your children:

1 They are children.

2 They will tend to act like children.

3 Much childish behavior is unpleasant.

4 If I do my part as a parent and love them, despite their childish behavior, they will mature and give up their childish ways.

5 If I love them only when they please me (conditional love), and if I express my love to them only at those times, they will not feel genuinely loved. This will damage their self-image, make them feel insecure, and actually prevent them from moving into better self-control and more mature behavior. Therefore, their development and behavior is as much my responsibility as it is theirs.

6 If I love them only when they meet my requirements or expectations, they will feel incompetent and will believe it is pointless to do their best, since it is never enough. They will always be plagued by insecurity, anxiety, low self-esteem, and anger. To guard against this, I need to often remind myself of my responsibility for their total growth.

7 If I love them unconditionally, they will feel comfortable about themselves and will be able to control their anxiety and their behavior as they grow to adulthood.

Of course, there are age-appropriate behaviors with our sons and daughters. Teens act differently than little children, and a thirteen-year-old will respond differently than a seven-year-old. But we must remember they are still minors, not mature adults, so we can expect them to fail at times. Show patience with them as they learn to grow.

WHAT YOUR CHILD NEEDS FROM YOU

This book focuses primarily on our children's need for love and how to provide it. That's because it is their greatest emotional need and greatly affects our relationship with them. Other needs, especially physical needs, are easier to recognize and usually easier to fulfill, but they are not as satisfying or life-changing. Yes, we need to provide our children shelter, food, and clothing. But we are also responsible to foster the mental and emotional growth and health of our children.

We used to worry about "self-esteem." Then we sought to provide it in parenting, schooling, sports, all areas where adults were interacting with kids. Perhaps we were too successful! The child with an embellished sense of self will see himself as superior to others—as God's gift to the world and deserving of whatever he wants. Studies show this inflated sense of self-esteem is rampant among the young today. Psychology professor Jean Twenge notes that measures of self-esteem have risen consistently since the 1980s among children of all ages—and "what starts off as healthy self-esteem can quickly morph into an inflated view of oneself."[1]

But equally damaging, the child who underestimates his worth will struggle with thoughts such as, "I am not as smart, athletic, or beautiful as others." "I can't" is his theme song, and "I didn't" is his reality. It is worthy of our best efforts as parents to see that our children develop appropriate self-esteem so that they will view themselves as important members of society with special talents and abilities and will feel a desire to be productive.

Children also have a universal need for *security and safety*. In our world of uncertainties, at home and "out there," it is increasingly difficult for parents to provide this sense of security. At the same time, parents can't hover like the "helicopter parents" we've all heard of (and may worry we're turning into). As we said earlier, our task as parents is to raise mature adults capable of functioning and flourishing in the world.

A child needs to develop relational skills so that she will treat all persons as having equal value and will be able to build friendships through a balanced flow of giving and receiving. Without these skills, a child is in danger of becoming withdrawn and remaining that way into adulthood. A child lacking essential relational skills might also become a controlling bully who lacks empathy and treats others cruelly. Finally, a child must learn to relate properly to authority. Without this, no other abilities will mean very much.

Parents need to help their children nurture their special gifts and talents so that the children will feel the inner satisfaction and sense of accomplishment that come from using one's innate abilities. Conscientious parents must maintain the delicate balance between pushing and encouraging. (See *8 Great Smarts*, by Kathy Koch, PhD, for more on this.)

Your children will sense how you feel about them by how you behave toward them. If you began to list all the behavioral ways to love a child, I doubt that you could fill more than one page. There just aren't that many ways, and that is fine, because you want to keep it simple. What matters is to keep your children's love tanks full. You can simply remember that behavioral expressions of love can be divided into physical touch, quality time, gifts, acts of service, and words of affirmation.

Beginning with chapter 2, we will help you uncover your child's primary love language. If your child is under age four, speak all five languages. Tender touch, supporting words, quality time, gifts, and acts of service all converge to meet your child's need for love. If that need is met and your child genuinely feels loved, it will be far easier for him to learn and respond in other areas. This love interfaces with all other needs a child has. Speak all five languages when your child is older, too, for he needs all five to grow, even though he craves one more than the others.

When you discover your child's love language and thus she receives the love she needs, don't assume everything in her life will be problem-free. There will still be setbacks and misunderstandings. But your child, like a flower, will benefit from your love. When the water of love is given, your child will bloom and bless the world with beauty. Without that love, she will become a wilted flower, begging for water.

Because you want your children to grow into full maturity, you will want to show them love in all the languages and then teach them how to use these for themselves. The value is not only for your children but for the people with whom they will live and associate. One mark of a mature adult is the ability to give and receive appreciation through all the love languages—physical touch, quality time, words of affirmation, gifts, and acts of service. Few adults are able to do this; most of them give or receive love in one or two ways.

If this is not something you have done in the past, you may find that you too are changing and growing in understanding and in the quality of your relationships. In time, you will have a truly multilingual family.

2

LOVE LANGUAGE #1:

Physical Touch

Samantha is a fifth-grader whose family recently moved to a new community. "It's been hard this year, moving and having to make new friends. Back at my old school, I knew everybody and they knew me." When we asked if she ever felt as if her parents didn't love her because they took her away from her old school and town, Samantha said, "Oh no, I never felt they did this on purpose. I know they love me, because they always give me lots of extra hugs and kisses. I wish we hadn't had to move, but I know Daddy's job is important."

Samantha's love language is physical touch; those touches tell her Mom and Dad love her. Hugs and kisses are the most common way of speaking this love language, but there are other ways, too. A dad tosses his year-old son in the air. He spins his seven-year-old daughter round and round, and she laughs wildly. A mom reads a story with her three-year-old on her lap.

Such touching activities happen between parents and children, but not as often as you may think. Studies indicate that many parents touch their children only when it is necessary: when they are dressing or undressing them, putting them in the car, or carrying them to bed. It seems that many parents are unaware of how much their children need to be touched and how easily they can use this means to keep their children's emotional tanks filled with unconditional love.

Physical touch is the easiest love language to use unconditionally.

Physical touch is the easiest love language to use unconditionally, because parents need no special occasion or excuse to make physical contact. They have almost constant opportunity to transfer love to the heart of a child with touch. The language of touch is not confined to a hug or a kiss but includes any kind of physical contact. Even when they are busy, parents can often gently touch a child on the back, arm, or shoulder.

Though some parents are quite demonstrative, others almost try to avoid touching their children. Often this limited physical touching occurs because parents simply do not realize their pattern or do not know how to change it. Many are glad to learn how they can show love in this most basic way.

A DAD LEARNS ABOUT TOUCH

Chris was worried about his relationship with his four-year-old daughter, Audrey, because she was pulling away from him and seemed to avoid being with him. Chris had a big heart, but he was very reserved and usually kept his feelings to himself. He had always felt uncomfortable in expressing his emotions through physical touch. Because he wanted so much to be close to Audrey, he was willing to make some changes, and began showing love to her with a light touch on her arm, back, or shoulders. Gradually he increased his use of this love language and eventually could hug and kiss his precious daughter without feeling uncomfortable.

This change wasn't easy for Chris, but as he became more demonstrative, he discovered that Audrey needed extraordinary amounts of paternal affection. If she didn't receive it, she would become angry and upset. Chris came to understand how a lack of affection on his part could distort Audrey's relationships with all males later on.

Chris found out the power of this particular love language. In recent years, many research studies have come to the same conclusion: Babies who are held, caressed, and kissed develop a healthier emotional life than those who are left for long periods of time without physical contact, such as infants in overseas orphanages.

Physical touch is one of love's strongest voices. It shouts, "I love you!" The importance of touching children is not a modern notion. In the first century AD, the Hebrews living in Palestine brought their children to Jesus "that He might touch them."[1] The writer Mark reported that the disciples of Jesus rebuked the parents, thinking their teacher was too busy with "important" matters to spend time on children. But Jesus was indignant with His disciples. "'Let the little children come to me, and do not hinder them, for the kingdom of God belongs to such as these. Truly I tell you, anyone who will not receive the kingdom of God like a little child will never enter it.' And he took the children in his arms, placed his hands on them and blessed them."[2]

You will learn to spot your child's primary language in chapter 7. It may not be physical touch—but that does not matter. All children need to be touched, and wise parents in many cultures recognize the importance of touching their children. They also recognize the need to have their children receive the tender touch of other significant adults, such as grandparents.

TOUCH THROUGH THE GROWING YEARS

Infants and Toddlers

Our children need plenty of touches during their first few years. Fortunately, to hold and cuddle an infant seems almost instinctual for mothers, and in most cultures fathers also actively participate in giving affection.

But in busy America, parents sometimes do not touch children as much as they should. They work long hours and often come home tired. If a mother works, she should be sure the caregiver is free and able to touch. Will the child be lovingly touched throughout the day or left to lie in a crib alone, unattended, and unloved? In childcare, a baby deserves loving and gentle touches whether in changing diapers or during feeding or carrying. Even an infant is able to tell the difference between gentle and harsh or irritating touches. Parents should make every effort to ensure the loving treatment of their children during the hours they are apart.

As a baby grows and becomes more active, the need for touch does not lessen. Hugs and kisses, wrestling on the floor, riding piggyback, and other playful loving touches are vital to the child's emotional development. Children need many meaningful touches every day, and parents should make every effort to provide these expressions of love. If you are not naturally a "hugger," you may feel that you're consciously going against your natural tendency. But you can learn. When we come to understand the importance of lovingly touching our children, we are motivated to change.

Boys and girls alike need physical affection, yet young boys often receive less than young girls. There are many reasons for this, but the most common is that some parents feel that physical affection will somehow feminize a boy. Of course, this is not true. The fact is that the more parents keep the emotional tank full, the healthier the child's self-esteem and sexual identity will be.

School-Age Children

When your child begins school, he still has a strong need for physical touch. A hug given as he leaves each morning may be the difference between emotional security and insecurity throughout the day. A hug when the child returns home may determine whether your child has a quiet evening of positive mental and physical activity or makes a rambunctious effort to get your attention. Why is this? Children are facing new experiences at school each day and they feel both positive and negative emotions toward teachers and peers. Therefore, home should be a haven, the place where love is secure. Remember, physical touch is one of love's strong languages. As it is spoken in a natural and loving way, your child becomes more comfortable and has an easier time communicating with other people.

But I have a couple of boys, and as they grow older, they have less need for affection and especially for physical touch, some may argue. Not so! *All* children need physical contact throughout their childhood and adolescence. Many boys from age seven to nine go through a stage when they are resistant to affectionate touch, and yet they still need physical contact. They tend to be responsive to more vigorous contact such as wrestling, jostling, playful hitting, bear hugs, high fives, and the like. Girls also enjoy this type of physical touch, but they do not resist the softer touches as well, for unlike boys, they do not go through the affection-resistant stage.

Much physical touch at this stage in a child's life will come through playing games. Basketball, football, and soccer are all contact sports. When you are playing games together in the backyard, you are combining both quality time and physical touch. But touch should not be limited to such play. Running your hand through your child's hair, touching him on the shoulder or arm, patting him on the back or leg, along with some encouraging words, are all meaningful expressions of love to a growing child.

A favorite kind of physical touch for many parents is to hold a small child while reading a story. This enables parents to maintain the touch for longer periods of time, something deeply meaningful to the child that becomes a lifelong memory.

Other times when physical touch is important are when a child is sick, hurt physically or emotionally, tired, or when something funny or sad has taken place. Parents need to make sure that they treat boys in the same way they do girls at such times. Most boys tend to consider physical affection as "feminine" in some periods of their development; when they are resistant, it is easier for parents to keep more distance from them. Also, some adults regard boys as less appealing during certain stages. If parents experience such feelings, it is important to resist them; go ahead and give boys the physical touch they need, even if they act as if they don't want it.

From Tweens to Teens

During your child's grade school years, it is essential to remember that you are preparing him or her for the most difficult part of childhood—adolescence. When a child is small, it is comparatively easy to fill the emotional tank. Of course, it becomes empty very fast and must be replenished. As the child grows, the emotional love tank also grows and keeping it full becomes more difficult. Eventually that boy will be bigger than you, and stronger and smarter—just ask him! And your daughter will become a wonderful adultlike person who is brighter and smarter than you are!

Continue to fuel their tanks with love, even when they may not give you signs of their needs. While boys approaching adolescence may pull back from touch, fearing it's too feminine, girls may find their fathers pulling back. If you want to properly prepare your preadolescent daughter for the future, don't hold back with the touches. Here's why.

During the preadolescent stage, girls have a particular need for expressions of love from their fathers. Unlike boys, the importance of being assured of unconditional love increases for girls and seems to reach a zenith around the age of eleven. One reason for this special need is that mothers generally provide more physical affection at this stage than fathers do.

If you could watch a group of sixth-grade girls at school, you would see the difference between those who are prepared for adolescence and those who are struggling. As a girl nears this delicate stage in her life, she intuitively knows that she needs to feel good about herself. She also unconsciously knows that she needs to have a good sexual identity in order to weather the years ahead. It is crucial that she feel valuable as a female.

As you watch the girls, you will see that some have a difficult time relating to the opposite sex. They are either shy or withdrawn around boys, or they may be flirtatious and even seductive. While boys may enjoy the flirtations of an attractive girl, they do not hold her in high regard and usually ridicule her in private. But the real agony for this girl is not just her reputation but her ongoing relationships with other girls. They tend to resent her because of her behavior with boys. At this age, having normal and supportive friendships with other girls is far more important than getting along with boys. These friendships also set a lifelong pattern.

Some of those girls you observe do not resort to awkward behavior with boys. They can simply be themselves because of their healthy self-esteem and sexual identity. Their behavioral patterns are consistent and stable, whether they are interacting with the star quarterback or a shy, hesitant boy. You also notice that the boys hold them in high esteem. But best of all, they have close, supportive, meaningful relationships with other girls.

Girls with strong and healthy self-esteem and sexual identity can better stand against negative peer pressure. They are more able to hold on to the moral standards they were taught at home, and are better equipped to think for themselves.

What makes the difference in these girls? Some have such problems with their peer relationships and others are doing beautifully. You guessed it—the emotional love tank. Most of those who are doing well have fathers who take their part in keeping the emotional tank full. But if a girl does not have a father present in the home, all is not lost. She may find a good father substitute in a grandfather or uncle. Many fatherless girls grow to be healthy women in every way.

THE DARK SIDE OF TOUCH

It is sad but true that not all touch is loving. It seems that almost daily we hear some story about a teacher or coach or relative or, yes, religious leader who has been accused of inappropriate touch. Some of us lament the passing of a time when a teacher could freely hug one of her pupils. However, the trauma endured by those who have suffered sexual abuse (or angry physical abuse) is not to be minimized. A discussion of "inappropriate" touch is beyond the scope of this book. But if you are interested in exploring this issue further, there is a wealth of resources available. I highly recommend *Helping Victims of Sexual Abuse*, by Lynn Heitritter and Jeanette Vought, as an excellent overview of this sensitive topic.

WHEN YOUR CHILD'S PRIMARY LOVE LANGUAGE IS TOUCH

Is your child's primary love language touch? Be sure to read chapter 7 to determine for sure. However, here are some clues. For children who understand this love language, physical touch will communicate love more deeply than will the words "I love you," or giving a present, fixing a bicycle, or spending time with them. Of course, they receive love in all the languages, but for them the one with the clearest and loudest voice is physical touch. Without hugs, kisses, pats on the back, and other physical expressions of love, their love tanks will remain less than full.

When you use physical touch with these children, your message of love will come through loud and clear. A tender hug communicates love to any child, but it shouts love to these children. Conversely, if you use physical touch as an expression of anger or hostility, you will hurt these children very deeply. A slap in the face is detrimental to any child, but it is devastating to children whose primary love language is touch.

Michelle didn't learn about the five love languages until her son Jaden was twelve years old. At the end of a love languages seminar, she turned to a friend and said, "Now I finally understand Jaden. For years he has annoyed me by constantly picking at me. When I'm working at the computer, he walks up behind me, puts his hands around my face and covers my eyes. If I walk past him, he reaches out and pinches my arm. If I walk through the room when he's lying on the floor, he grabs my leg. Sometimes he pulls my arms behind me. He used to run his hands through my hair when I was sitting on the couch, although he doesn't anymore since I told him to keep his hands out of my hair. He does the same thing to his father, and the two of them usually end up in a wrestling match on the floor.

"Now I realize that Jaden's primary love language is physical touch. All these years, he has been touching me because he wants to *be* touched. I admit that I'm not much of a toucher—my parents were not hugging people. I now realize that my husband has been loving Jaden with his wrestling, while I have been drawing back from his efforts to get love from me. How could I have missed it all this time—it seems so simple now."

That night Michelle talked with her husband about the seminar. William was somewhat surprised by what he heard. "I hadn't thought of the wrestling as love, but that makes a lot of sense," he told his wife. "I was just doing what came naturally for me. And you know, physical touch is my primary love language too."

When Michelle heard this, another light went on. No wonder William was always wanting to hug and kiss! Even when he wasn't interested in sex, he was the "touchiest" person she had ever met. That night Michelle felt as if she had almost too many new things to think about, and yet she determined to learn to speak the love language of physical touch. She would start by simply responding to their touches.

The next time Jaden came by where she was sitting at the computer and put his hands over her eyes, she rose, turned, and gave him a bear hug. Jaden was surprised, but he laughed. And the next time William put his arms around her, she responded the way she did when they were dating. He smiled and said, "I'm going to send you to more seminars. This stuff really works!"

Michelle persisted in her efforts to learn a new love language and, in due time, touching began to feel more comfortable for her. But long before she felt fully comfortable, William and Jaden were reaping the benefits of her physical touches and were responding to her by speaking her primary love language, acts of service. Jaden was picking up after himself and William was vacuuming, and Michelle thought she'd gone to heaven.

WHAT THE CHILDREN SAY

For many children, physical touch speaks louder than words, gifts, quality time, or acts of service. Without it, their love tank will never be overflowing. Look at what these children had to say about the power of physical touch.

Stella, age seven: "I know my mommy loves me because she hugs me."

Jeremy, a junior in college, told us how he knew his parents loved him: "They showed it all the time. Every time I left the house as long as I can remember, I always got a hug and kiss from my mom and a hug from my dad, if he was home. And every time I came home, it was a repeat performance. It's still that way. Some of my friends can't believe my parents, because they didn't grow up in touching families, but I like it. I still look forward to their hugs. It gives me warm feelings inside."

Eleven-year-old Hunter was asked, "On a zero-to-ten scale, how much do your parents love you?" Without batting an eye he answered, "Ten." When we asked why he felt this so strongly, he said, "Well, for one thing because they tell me, but even more from the way they treat me. Dad is always bumping me when he walks by, and we wrestle on the floor. He's a lot of fun. And Mom's always hugging me, although she has stopped doing it in front of my friends."

Taylor, twelve, lives with her mother most of the time and visits with her father every other weekend. She said that she feels especially loved by her father. When we asked why, she said, "Because every time I go to see him, he hugs and kisses me and tells me how glad he is to see me. When I leave, he hugs me for a long time and tells me he misses me. I know my mom loves me too—she does lots of things for me—but I wish she would hug me and act as excited about being with me as Daddy does."

If physical touch is your child's primary love language and you are not by nature a toucher and yet want to learn your child's love language, it may help if you begin by touching yourself. Yes, we're serious. First, take your hand and touch your arm, beginning at the wrist and working slowly up to your shoulder. Give yourself a shoulder rub. Now take the other hand and do the same thing on the other side. Run both hands through your hair, massaging your scalp as you work from front to back. Sit up straight with both feet on the floor and pat your legs—with rhythm if you want. Place one hand on your stomach. Then lean over and touch your feet and massage your ankles. Sit up and say, "There, I did it. I touched myself, and I can touch my child!"

For those who have never been touched and find touching uncomfortable, this exercise can be a first step in breaking down barriers to physical touch. If you are one of these people, you may want to repeat this exercise once a day until you have enough courage to initiate a touch to your child or spouse. Once you get started, set a goal and consciously touch your child every day. Later, you can work up to several touches a day. Anyone can learn the language of physical touch, and if it is your child's primary love language, it is worth your best efforts.

Here are a few more ideas especially for parents. Pick and choose among them to try something new you think your child will appreciate.

- When you greet or say goodbye to your young child, gather them into your arms and hold them. Kneel down for small children.

- Let your child hold or cuddle a soft item, such as a blanket to soothe them.

- Hug and kiss your child every day when they leave and return from school, as well as when you tuck them in at night for younger children.

- Stroke your child's hair or rub their back when they tell you about a difficult day or are upset.

- Shortly after disciplining your child, take a moment to give them a hug to show them the discipline was based on the consequences of their wrongful choices but that you still love and cherish them as your child.

- Snuggle closely together on the couch when watching television together.

- Give each other a high five or similar congratulations whenever you catch your child doing something positive.

- Purchase a gift for your child that is touch-oriented, such as a soft pillow, blanket, or sweater.

- Occasionally yell out a "group hug" for your entire family, regardless of how small or large the family size. To add more fun, include family pets such as the dog or cat.

- Play games or sports together that require physical touch. This will allow both shared time together and touch that is meaningful without appearing forced.

- Sing action songs together with your children that require touching and action, such as clapping hands, spinning, or jumping. Many of today's children's DVDs make this even easier.

- Have "tickle fights" with your children, being careful not to allow it to become a stressful activity for your child.

- With younger children, read stories together with your child on your lap.

- When your child is sick or gets hurt, spend extra time providing comfort, like wiping her face with a cool cloth.

- Hold hands during family prayers.

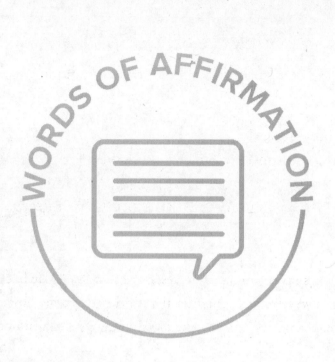

WORDS OF AFFIRMATION

3

LOVE LANGUAGE #2:

Words of Affirmation

D oes my father love me? Yes, because when I play hockey, he always cheers, and after the game he tells me, 'Thanks for playing hard.' He says that the main thing is not to win but to do my best."

Sam, age eleven, continued. "Sometimes I make mistakes, but he tells me not to worry. He says I'll do better if I keep on doing my best."

In communicating love, words are powerful. Words of affection and endearment, words of praise and encouragement, words that give positive guidance all say, "I care about you." Such words are like a gentle, warm rain falling on the soul; they nurture the child's inner sense of worth and security. Even though such words are quickly said, they are not soon forgotten. A child reaps the benefits of affirming words for a lifetime.

Conversely, cutting words, spoken out of short-lived frustration, can hurt a child's self-esteem and cast doubts about his abilities. Children think we deeply believe what we say. The ancient Hebrew proverb did not overstate the reality: "The tongue has the power of life and death."[1]

The second love language is *words of affirmation.* Some children feel their greatest sense of love in expressions that affirm them. These expressions need not be the words "I love you," as we will see.

UNDERSTANDING "I LOVE YOU"

Long before they can understand the meanings of words, children receive emotional messages. The tone of voice, the gentleness of mood, the sense of caring all communicate emotional warmth and love. All parents talk to their infants, and what the babies understand is the look on the face and the affection-ate sounds, combined with physical closeness.

Children think we deeply believe what we say.

Because young children grow gradually in their ability to use words and concepts, they will not always know what we mean by our words, even when we say, "I love you." Love is an abstract concept. They can't see love as they can see a toy or a book. Because children tend to think concretely, we need to help them understand what we mean when we express our love. The words "I love you" take on greater meaning when the child can associate them with your affectionate feelings, and often this means physical closeness. For instance, when you are reading to a child at bedtime, holding your little one close, at a point in the story where the child's feelings are warm and loving, you can softly say, "I love you, Honey."

Once your child begins to understand what your "I love you" means, you can use these words in different ways and times, so that they become connected to regular events, such as sending a child off to play or to school. Also, you can combine your words of love with genuine praise for something about your child. Kathleen, now a mother of two, says, "I remember how my mother used to talk about my beautiful red hair. Her positive comments as she combed my hair before school have been a constant part of my self-perception. Years later when I discovered that we redheads are in the minority, I never had negative feelings about my red hair. I'm sure my mother's loving comments had a lot to do with that."

THE RIGHT KIND OF PRAISE

Praise and affection are often combined in the messages we give to a child. We need to distinguish the two. Affection and love mean *expressing appreciation for the very being of a child,* for those characteristics and abilities that are part of the total package of the person. In contrast, we express *praise for what the child does,* either in achievements or behavior or conscious attitudes. Praise, as we are using it here, is for something over which the child has a degree of control.

Because you want words of praise to be genuinely meaningful to your child, you need to be careful about what you say. If you use praise too frequently, your words will have little positive effect. For example, you may say something like, "You are a good girl." Those are wonderful words, but you need to be wise in using them. It is more effective to say this when the child has done something for which she feels good and would expect a compliment. This is especially true with specific compliments such as, "Great catch!" when it was just an average catch. Children know when praise is given for justified reasons and when it is given simply to make them feel good, and they may interpret the latter as insincere.

Frequent random praise is risky for another reason. Some children become so accustomed to this type of praise that they assume it is natural and they come to expect it. When they are in situations where such praise is not given, they assume something is wrong with them and they become anxious. When they see other children who do not receive such bolstering, they can wonder why they feel such excessive need of praise.

Of course, we want to praise children we care about, but we want to make sure that the praise is both true and justified. Otherwise they may regard it as flattery, which they can equate with lying.

THE POWER OF ENCOURAGEMENT

The word *encourage* means "to instill courage." We are seeking to give children the courage to attempt more. To a young child, almost every experience is new. Learning to walk, to talk, or to ride a bicycle requires constant courage. By our words, we either encourage or discourage the child's efforts.

Speech pathologists say that children learn to speak by mimicking adults, but that the process is enhanced if the adults not only pronounce the words clearly but also give verbal encouragement to the child's struggling attempts to say them correctly. Statements such as, "That's close, that's good, yes, great, you've got it," encourage the child not only in learning the words at hand but also in developing future vocabulary.

> The greatest enemy of encouraging our children is anger.

The same principle is true in the child's learning of social skills. "I saw how you shared your toys with Madison. I like that—life is much easier when we share." Words such as these give a child that added inner motivation to go against what might be a natural desire to hoard. Or consider a parent who says to a sixth-grader,

"Danny, I noticed that tonight after the game you were listening closely to Ravi as he shared his feelings about his game. I was so proud of you for giving him your undivided attention, even though others were slapping you on the back as they walked by. Listening to people is one of the greatest gifts you can give them." This parent is instilling in Danny the courage to develop the art of listening, one of the most important arts in the field of human relationships.

Maybe you find it difficult to use encouraging words. Keep in mind that one aspect of feeling encouraged is feeling good physically. Exuberance and vitality require energy; this means as parents we need to be in the best possible health physically, mentally, emotionally, and spiritually. When we feel encouraged, we are better able to encourage our children. In two-parent households, the parents should encourage one another; if you're a single parent, have trusted friends or relatives who will bolster your spirits and energy.

The greatest enemy of encouraging our children is anger. The more anger the parent harbors, the more anger the parent will dump on the children. The result will be children who are both anti-authority and anti-parent. This naturally means that a thoughtful parent will do all in his or her power to assuage anger—to keep it to a minimum and to handle it maturely.

The writer of Proverbs is wise indeed: "A gentle answer turns away wrath."[2] The volume of a parent's voice has great influence over a child's reaction to what the parent says. It takes practice to speak softly, but we can all learn how to do it. Also, when we are feeling tense with our children, we can learn to speak calmly, asking questions whenever possible, rather than issuing commands. For example, which of these statements would best encourage a child or teenager? "Take out the garbage now!" or "Would you take out the garbage for me, please?"

When we try to encourage our children in a particular matter, they will more likely respond favorably rather than reject our ideas.

WHAT MARK TOOK TO WAR

Years ago a middle-school teacher in Minnesota did a remarkable thing. She asked her students to list the names of all the other students in the class, leaving a space between names. Then she told them to think of the nicest thing they could say about each of their classmates and write it down. At the end of the period she collected these sheets and over the weekend, she wrote the name of each student on a separate sheet and listed what everyone had said about that person. On Monday, she gave each student his or her list.

As they began reading, they started whispering to each other, "I never knew that meant anything to anyone" or, "I didn't know others liked me so much." The papers were never discussed in class, but the teacher knew the exercise was a success because it gave her students such a positive feeling about themselves.

Several years later, one of those students was killed in Vietnam. After his body was returned to Minnesota, most of his classmates, along with the math teacher, attended the funeral. At the luncheon after the service, the father of the young man said to the teacher, "I want to show you something," and took a wallet out of his pocket. "They found this on Mark when he was killed. We thought you might recognize it." Opening the billfold, he removed two worn sheets of notebook paper that had been taped, folded, and refolded many times. It was the list of good things Mark's classmates had written about him.

"Thank you so much for doing that," Mark's mother told the teacher. "As you can see, our son treasured it." One by one, Mark's classmates began to reveal that each of them still had their sheet and that they read it often. Some carried it in a billfold; one had even put it in his wedding album. One man said, "I think we all saved our list."[3]

RIGHT MESSAGE, WRONG MANNER

Encouraging words are most effective when they are focused on a specific effort your child has made. The goal is to catch your child doing something good and then commend him for it. Yes, this takes far more effort than catching your child doing something wrong and then condemning him for it, but the end result is worth it: direction that guides your child in his moral and ethical development.

Children need guidance. They learn to speak by being exposed to a particular language. They learn how to behave by living in a certain kind of society. In most cultures, parents have the primary responsibility for social- izing children. This involves not only the social dos and don'ts but also their ethical and moral development.

Many parents view parental guidance as an exercise in prohibition.

All children are guided by someone. If you as their parents are not their primary guides, then other influences and individuals assume that role—school, media, the culture, other adults, or peers who are getting their guidance from someone else. Ask yourself this ques- tion: *are my children receiving positive and loving guidance?* Loving guidance always has a child's best interests in mind. Its purpose is not to make parents and other adults look good; its purpose is to help the child develop the qualities that will serve him well in the future. The fourth type of affirming words offers your child guidance for the future. It's a powerful element of the second love language.

Too often parents give the right message but in the wrong manner.

They tell their children to stay away from drinking, but their harsh and cruel manner may in fact drive the children to alcohol. Words of guidance must be given in a positive way. A positive message delivered in a negative manner will always reap negative results. As one child said, "My parents are yelling and screaming at me, telling me not to yell and scream. They expect me to do something they have not learned to do. It's unfair."

Another difficulty is that many parents view parental guidance as an exercise in prohibition. "Don't lie." "Don't hit your sister." "Don't cross the street." "Don't eat too much candy." Then, later: "Don't drink and drive." "Don't get pregnant." "Don't smoke." "Don't experiment with drugs." "Don't go to that concert." These are all good warnings but hardly enough direction to build a meaningful life. To be sure, prohibition is part of parental guidance, but it should never be the predominant element. In the biblical account of the Garden of Eden, God gave Adam and Eve only one negative; all other guidance was positive. He gave them meaningful work to fill their lives with productive activity. Much later, when the children of Israel came to Sinai, they were given the Ten Commandments, which include both positive and negative commands. In Jesus' Sermon on the Mount, His guidance is overwhelmingly positive.

The negative is necessary, but only as a part of the guidance we give our children. The supreme law is the law of love, and it is loving, positive guidance that our children so desperately need. If we can guide them into positive, meaningful pursuits, they are less likely to fall prey to the perils we want them to avoid.

Parents who offer words of loving guidance will be looking closely at the interests and abilities of their children and giving positive verbal reinforcement of those interests. From academic pursuits to simple rules of etiquette to the complex art of personal relationships, parents need to be expressing emotional love in the positive verbal guidance they give their children.

When your son or daughter is a teen, rather than condemning your child's friends who are making poor choices, it is far better to take a loving approach that expresses concern for them. You might show your child accounts of accidents and deaths that involve drugs and alcohol and share how painful it is for you to think about such devastation in the lives of these young people and their families. When your child hears your loving expressions of concern for other young people, he is far more likely to identify with you than when he hears you condemning people who do such things.

WHEN YOUR CHILD'S PRIMARY LOVE LANGUAGE IS WORDS OF AFFIRMATION

The words "I love you" should always stand alone in reality or by implication. To say, "I love you . . . will you please do this for me?" dilutes the theme of love. To say, "I love you, but I'll tell you right now . . ." cancels itself out. The words "I love you" should never be diluted with conditional statements. This is true for all children, but especially for those whose primary love language is words.

To his parents, ten-year-old Cole seemed very lethargic. They had tried all sorts of things to help him be more interested in life— from sports to a dog—and they were at their wits' end. They often complained to Cole about his attitude, telling him that he should be thankful to have parents who cared about him and also that he needed to find an interest he could develop. They even threatened to take him to a counselor if he didn't get more excited about life.

After Steve and Jen attended a seminar about the love languages, they wondered immediately if Cole's primary love language might be words of affirmation. They realized that this was the one thing they had not given him. Instead, they had showered him with gifts, hugged him daily, and provided quality time and acts of service. But their actual words to their son sent another message—one of criticism.

So they developed a plan. Jen and Steve began to make a conscious effort to give Cole words of affirmation, starting with comments about what they liked about him. As they prepared for this experiment, they decided that for one month they would concentrate on making their words communicate the message, "We care about you, we love you, we like you."

Cole was a physically attractive child, and so they would begin by commenting on his appearance. They would not tie their words of affirmation to a suggestion such as, "You're strong—you should be playing football." Rather they would talk about his athletic build and leave it at that. They also began to watch for things in Cole's behavior that pleased them and then made positive statements. If he fed their terrier, Lucy, they expressed appreciation rather than saying, "It's about time." When they had to give guidance, they would try to keep it positive.

A month later Steve and Jen reported, "We can't believe the change in Cole. He's a different kid . . . maybe because we're different parents. His attitude toward life is much more positive. He's sharing jokes with us and laughing. He is feeding Lucy and was recently out playing football with some kids. We think we're on the right track."

Steve and Jen's discovery changed them as well as Cole. They learned that parenting is not just a matter of doing what comes naturally. Because every child is different, it is essential to communicate love to that child in his or her primary language. Jen and Steve's story shows that it is possible to use a child's love language wrongly, bringing hurt and frustration to the child. Cole's language was words of affirmation—and they were giving him words of condemnation. Such words are harmful to any child, but they are extremely destructive to a child whose primary language is words of affirmation.

If you think this is your child's language, and yet you have a hard time saying affirming things, we suggest that you keep a notebook titled "Words of Affirmation." When you hear other parents giving affirmation to their children, write their statements in your notebook. When you read an article on childrearing, record the positive words you find. Look for books on parent–child relationships and record all the words of affirmation you discover. Then practice saying those words in front of a mirror. The more often you say them, the more they will become your own. Then consciously look for opportunities to say these affirming things to your child, at least three times a day.

If you find that you fall back into old patterns of condemnation or negativism, tell your child that you are sorry, that you realize the words are hurtful, and this is not how you feel about him. Ask him to forgive you. Tell him that you are trying to become a better parent and that you love him very deeply and want to communicate that love more effectively. In due time, you will be able to break the old habits and establish new patterns. The best reward of all is that you will see the effect on the face of your child, especially in his eyes, and you will feel it in your heart. And the chances are good that you will begin to receive words of affirmation from him; the more he feels loved by you, the more he is likely to reciprocate.

WHAT THE CHILDREN SAY

The following four children share words of affirmation as their primary love language.

Melissa, eight, said, "I love my mother because she loves me. Every day she tells me that she loves me. I think my father does too, but he never tells me so."

Grace, age twelve, broke her arm this year. "I know that my parents love me because while I was having such a hard time keeping up with my schoolwork, they encouraged me. They never forced me to do homework when I wasn't feeling well, but told me I could do it later. They said how proud they were that I was trying so hard and that they knew I would be able to keep up."

Jacob is an active, outspoken five-year-old, confident that his parents love him. "My mommy loves me and my daddy loves me. Every day they say, 'I love you.'"

John, ten, has been in foster homes since he was three. For the past eight months he has lived with Doug and Betsy, his fourth set of foster parents. When he was asked if they genuinely loved him, he said they did. We asked why he said that so quickly. "Because they don't yell and scream at me. My last foster parents yelled and screamed all the time. They treated me like trash. Doug and Betsy treat me like a person. I know I have lots of problems, but I also know that they love me."

For children whose primary love language is words of affirmation, nothing is more important to their sense of being loved than to hear parents and other adults verbally affirm them. But the reverse is also true—words of condemnation will hurt them very deeply. Harsh and critical words are detrimental to all children, but to those whose primary language is words of affirmation, such negative words are devastating. And they can play those words in their minds for many years.

Thus, it is essential for parents and other significant adults in the child's life to quickly apologize for negative, critical, or harsh remarks. While the words can't be erased by an apology, their effect can be minimized. If you realize that you have a negative communication pattern with your child, you might encourage your spouse to record some of your episodes so that you can hear yourself. This can be very sobering, but it can also be a step in breaking negative patterns of speaking. Because positive communication is so important to every successful parent–child relationship, it is worth the effort to break old patterns and establish new ones. The benefit to your child will be enormous, and the sense of satisfaction you gain will be very rewarding.

IF YOUR CHILD'S LOVE LANGUAGE IS
WORDS OF AFFIRMATION:

Here are a few more ideas especially for parents. Pick and choose among them to try something new you think your child will appreciate.

- Put a Post-it note in their lunchbox with some encouraging words.

- Make a habit of mentioning something specific you've observed that highlights your child's accomplishments. Examples include: "I really appreciated how you showed kindness to that other child," or "I liked the positive attitude you had during the game."

- Ask what your child wants to do or be when they grow up. Then encourage them in ways that help them pursue these dreams. If your daughter says, "I want to be a veterinarian when I grow up," say things like, "I think you'd be a good vet."

- Send your older child a text message telling them how much they mean to you. Even better, make this a habit for when you have to go out of town or on a special holiday such as a birthday.

- If you are artistic, create a painting or drawing that shows how much you love your child.

- Take a picture or other creation your child has made and frame it with a note of why it means so much to you.

- Call your child at home whenever you think of them just to say, "I love you."

- Create a special name of affection for your child that is only used between the two of you.

- When you have to be out of town for work or other reasons, leave a series of short notes for your child, one for each day you are apart.

- Make it a habit to say, "I love you" whenever you tuck in your child or leave one another.

- Place their artwork in areas they recognize as important to you such as the refrigerator, the office, or special scrapbook.

- When your child is feeling down, share five reasons why you are proud of them.

- Leave a note on a cereal box, bathroom mirror, or other place you know your child will look. A simple "Daddy loves you," or "Mommy loves you," in a unique location can be very powerful.

- Get a picture key chain and put photos of your children in it. Talk about the photos with family or friends when your children are present.

- Create an encouragement jar that you and your child can use to drop in notes of praise and read together on a regular basis.

- Draw a large picture or words of encouragement using sidewalk chalk on your driveway, either together or as a surprise for them to see later.

- When a child makes a mistake trying to do something helpful, first use words to recognize that you knew of their good intentions.

QUALITY TIME

4

LOVE LANGUAGE #3:

Quality Time

Four-year-old Ella is pulling on her mother's leg. "Mommy, Mommy, let's go play!"

"I can't play right now," Kate says, staring at the screen. "I have to finish paying bills. I'll play with you after that. Go play by yourself for a few minutes and then we'll do something together."

In five minutes, Ella is back, begging to play. Kate responds, "Ellie, I told you that I have to do this one important thing first. Now run along and I'll be there in a few minutes." Ella leaves the room but in four minutes she is back. Eventually the bills are paid and the two have their playtime together. But Kate knows that the scenario will be repeated tomorrow.

What can we learn from Kate and Ella? The chances are good that little Ellie is revealing her primary love language—*quality time*. What really makes her feel loved is her mother's undivided attention. This is so important to her that she returns again and again. But Kate often sees these repeated requests as intrusions. If they persist long enough, she may even "lose it" with her daughter and send her to her room for an isolated time-out—just the opposite of what Ella needs.

What's the answer? Kate wonders. *Is it possible to love a child and still get my own work done?* The answer is a resounding yes. Learning a child's primary love language is one key to reaching that objective. If Kate had given Ella fifteen minutes of quality time *before* she started paying bills, she probably could have done her work in peace. When a child's love tank is empty and attention is the only thing that will fill it, that child will go to almost any length to get what she needs.

Even if your child's primary love language is not quality time, many children crave the undivided attention of parents. Indeed, much childhood misbehavior is an attempt to get more time with Mom or Dad. Even negative attention seems better than no attention to the child.

For years we have heard people talking about the need to give children "quality time," especially amidst the busyness of today's culture. And yet, while more people are talking about quality time, many children are starving for it.

Quality time is focused, undivided attention. Most infants receive plenty of quality time—feeding and changing alone offer that kind of attention, not only from mothers but fathers and perhaps extended family as well.

As a child grows, the giving of quality time becomes more difficult, because it requires real sacrifice on the part of parents. It's easier to give physical touch and words of affirmation than quality time. Few of us have enough hours in the day to get everything done as it is; giving a child quality time may mean that we have to give up something else. As children grow toward adolescence, they often need our attention just when we parents are exhausted, rushed, or emotionally out of sorts.

Quality time is a parent's gift of presence to a child. It conveys this message: "You are important. I like being with you." It makes the child feel that he is the most important person in the world to the parent. He feels truly loved because he has his parent all to himself.

When you spend quality time with children, you need to go to their physical/emotional level of development. When they are learning to crawl, for instance, you can sit on the floor with them. As they take their first steps, you should be nearby, urging them on. As they progress to sandboxes and learning to throw and kick a ball, you are there. When their world widens to include school, lessons of various sorts, sports, church, and community activities, you are all the while keeping up with them. The older a child is, the harder this may be, especially as you try to make private time for each child while staying involved in their more public activities.

> **Quality time does not require that you go somewhere special.**

"HE DOES THINGS WITH ME"

The most important factor in quality time is not the event itself but that you are doing something together, being together. When seven-year-old Nathan was asked how he knew his father loved him, he said, "Because he does things with me. Things like shooting baskets and playing games on the computer. And going to the pet store together."

Quality time does not require that you go somewhere special. You can provide focused attention almost anywhere, and your most nurturing quality times will often be at home, when you are alone with a child. Finding time to be alone with each child is not easy, and yet it is essential. In a society where people are increasingly spectators rather than participants, focused attention from parents is all the more critical.

In many homes, children would miss their computers and other electronic toys more than they would miss their fathers. Children are more and more influenced by forces outside the family and they need the strengthening influence of personal time with their parents. It takes real effort to carve out this kind of time in your schedule, and yet making the effort is rather like an investment in the future—of your children and your family.

If you have several children, you need to look for times when you can be alone with each one. This isn't easy, but it can be done. Consider Susanna Wesley, who raised ten children in eighteenth-century England. She scheduled an hour a week with each one alone. Her three sons, Sam, John, and Charles Wesley, became poets, writers, and preachers; Charles penned thousands of hymns, many of which remain classics in the Christian church. In addition to helping her children learn the alphabet, writing, and math, she taught them politeness and good manners, moral values, and frugal living.

> **Quality time not only means doing things together, it is a means for knowing your child better.**

In an era when women had little opportunity to use their gifts, Susanna prepared her daughters with a full education. The wise mother once told her daughter Emilia, "Society offers no opportunity for the intelligence of its women."[1] Emilia later became a teacher. While we don't necessarily advocate all of her ideas about raising children, we can admire the way Susanna set her priorities and then carried them through. The key to quality time is found in the values and priorities you as parents determine to cherish and implement in your home.

Positive Eye Contact

Quality time should include loving eye contact. Looking in your child's eyes with care is a powerful way to convey love from your heart to the heart of your child. Studies have shown that most parents use eye contact in primarily negative ways, either while reprimanding a child or giving very explicit instructions.

If you give loving looks only when your child is pleasing you, you are falling into the trap of conditional love. That can damage your ·child's personal growth. You want to give enough unconditional love to keep your child's emotional tank full, and a key way to do this is through proper use of eye contact.

Sometimes family members refuse to look at one another as a means of punishment. This is destructive to both adults and children. Kids especially interpret withdrawal of eye contact as disapproval, and this further erodes their self-esteem. Don't let your demonstration of love to a child be controlled by whether the child is pleasing you at the moment.

SHARING THOUGHTS AND FEELINGS

Quality time not only means *doing* things together, but it is a means for *knowing* your child better. As you spend time with your children, you will find that a natural result often is good conversation about everything related to your lives. Phil Briggs, longtime professor of education at a California seminary, loves the dividends of golfing with his son. "My son wasn't much of a talker until we started golfing together regularly." The Briggs's father–son twosome often talk about their game—the swing and other golf nuances—as they walk the fairways, but soon they get around to discussing other areas of life. When a parent shows a child how to throw a football or make pasta, he or she often creates an environment in which the parent and child can talk about more important issues.

Quality Conversations

This is when a father can reveal something of his own history, perhaps tell his child of his dating relationship with the boy's mother, and discuss moral and spiritual issues. This kind of "real" conversation communicates deeply to a child on an emotional level. It says, "My father trusts me. He cares. My father sees me as an important person and he loves me." A mother can mention her own fears about her appearance growing up as she helps her daughter shop for her first pair of glasses or a special dress for the prom. The conversation draws them together and helps the daughter understand that her value is not based on appearance.

Children never outgrow a need for quality conversation with parents and other adults. Such sharing of thoughts and feelings is the fabric of which life is made. Learning how to communicate on this level will serve them well in their own future relationships, including marriage. It will teach them how to build friendships and relate to work associates. It will show them how to process their own thoughts and to communicate in a positive, caring manner that respects the ideas of others. It will provide an example of how to disagree without being disagreeable.

Because your children will learn more from talking with you than you will probably ever realize, it is crucial that you spend time in healthy conversation with them, no matter what their age. If you limit your talking with them to correction, your children may never learn the value of positive, focused attention. Negative attention alone cannot meet their need for love.

With younger children, one of the most effective times to initiate conversation is at bedtime, when they are especially attentive. This may be because there are fewer distractions then or because the children want to delay going to bed. Whatever the reason, they are listening well and this makes meaningful conversation much easier.

"Read Me a Story"

All children love stories. Reading to them is a great way to begin your bedtime ritual—and do make it a ritual, because this will help to keep communications open when they become teenagers. During or after a story, you can pause to let a child identify his feelings about the events or characters and then talk about them. As you are reading a story about someone who experiences disappointment, for example, you may talk with your child about feelings of disappointment she has had, along with the accompanying sadness, anger, or whatever is appropriate.

We strongly recommend these times of conversation. Sadly, many young people today do not understand how to handle their feelings, especially anger. Many years of warm and close bedtime talks, which include gentle, relaxed sharing of feelings, can help prevent some of life's deepest problems down the road.

Bedtime rituals that are warm and close, gentle and relaxed, sound just the opposite of the busy world in which many parents live. Don't be a victim of the urgent. In the long run, much of what seems so pressing right now won't even matter. What you do with your children will matter forever.

PLANNING FOR QUALITY TIME

During the first eight years of a child's life, you can assume a fairly sane schedule, as the child's life centers primarily around the home. But as your child grows and becomes more involved in activities outside the home, you need to spend more time and effort preparing for family quality time. Otherwise it just won't happen. Here are several ideas.

First, mealtimes are natural events around which to plan. Over the years, a regular family dinner hour together can be one of the most bonding experiences that you will have. We all hear about families that just set out a pot of food and let everyone eat whenever they arrive home. To those who know the warmth and strength of a regular dinnertime together, year after year, this sounds chaotic. Parents are the only ones who can set the schedule for the family and decide when and if certain events will interrupt that schedule. Some families are able to have breakfast together. And, you may be able to meet a child for lunch once a month.

Second, consider overnight trips. Burney and his son, Jeff, do an overnighter every three months. They usually travel only an hour from home and camp out in their tent for a day and a half of uninterrupted time together. Allyson takes a walk two nights a week with her twelve-year-old daughter, Brittany. On those nights, her husband and son do the dishes and get some father/son time.

Third, simply riding along in the car as Mom or Dad runs errands or drives to a soccer game can result in quality conversation. There is something about sitting in a car that seems to bring out the desire to talk—and listen. Parents should be alert for those times when children seem to need to talk.

Those are just a few ideas. Remember, planning for your times together need not stifle spontaneity. You can always change your plans if you want to, but without making plans, you may find that you have little quality time with your children. You schedule other people into your calendars—why not your children? They will appreciate the fact that you value your time with them so much that you are willing to say no to other activities. And one by-product of planning is that you teach your children how to schedule their own time.

One of the most difficult times in a family's day can be when everyone returns from work and school, hungry and tired. So planning for time together also means preparing yourself. If you come home from a pressured workday, you need to release the stress of the day, clear your mind of things at work, and then focus on your home. Some people do this by playing their favorite music on the way home. Some friends we know stop the car near home and take a few minutes to pray. Find what will help you to feel relaxed and upbeat, so that you have the energy you need to give to your child.

If you cannot prepare yourself prior to arriving home, you and your spouse can work out a time for you to have to yourself, before you begin interacting with your children. You may need simply to change into comfortable clothes, open a Coke, and stroll in the backyard before settling in with the family. The more refreshed you are, the more you will be able to give to your family.

WHEN YOUR CHILD'S PRIMARY LOVE LANGUAGE IS QUALITY TIME

If quality time is your child's primary love language, you can be sure of this: without a sufficient supply of quality time and focused attention, your child will experience a gnawing uneasiness that his parents do not really love him.

Gerry was a firefighter who worked forty-eight hours on and twenty-four hours off. During his "on days," he stayed at the firehouse; when he was off, he and a fellow fireman often painted houses to make extra money. Meanwhile, his wife, Maggie, worked nights as a nurse and slept days. When both were working nights, their children, Jonathan, age eight, and Colleen, six, had their grandmother stay with them.

Gerry and Maggie became concerned about Jonathan, who over time seemed remote. Maggie later told a friend, "When we try to talk to him, he's very withdrawn-seeming. But when he was younger, he talked all the time.

"Before he started school and I was still home all the time, he and I would go to the park almost every afternoon. Now he's so different that it makes me wonder if something's wrong. Gerry doesn't notice it as much as I do, because he hasn't spent as much time with Jonathan, but I can see a big difference."

Maggie's friend Rosie had just been reading *The 5 Love Languages* and remembered the one chapter on how the love languages relate to children. So Rosie gave Maggie a copy and suggested that it might help her with Jonathan. Two weeks later Maggie told her friend, "I read the book and I think I know Jonathan's primary love language. Looking back and remembering how much he enjoyed our times together, and how talkative and excited he was, and then realizing that all that changed when he started school and I began work, I think the last two years he may have been almost starved for love. I've been meeting his physical needs but haven't been meeting his emotional needs very well."

The two women talked about how Maggie could work quality time with Jonathan into her schedule. Because her flexible time was afternoons and early evenings, she had been using that time for housework, shopping, an occasional night out with the girls, and a rare night out with Gerry. She also supervised Jonathan's homework. Maggie decided that if she tried, she could carve out an hour twice a week to spend concentrated time with Jonathan.

Three weeks later, Maggie told her friend, "It's working. Jonathan and I have had our hour twice a week since we last talked, and I'm seeing real change in his response to me. We decided to take our dog to the park one afternoon a week and out for tacos the other. Jonathan is beginning to talk more, and I can tell that he's responding emotionally to our time together.

"By the way, I've asked Gerry to read the book," Maggie added. "I think we need to learn to speak each other's love language. I know he's not speaking mine, and I don't think I'm speaking his either. Also, Gerry might see the importance of spending more time with Jonathan."

WHAT THE CHILDREN SAY

Here is how four children clearly reveal their primary love language to be quality time.

Eight-year-old Bethany has a twinkle in her eye most of the time. "I know my folks love me because they do things with me. Sometimes we all do stuff together, even with my little brother, but both of them do things just with me." When asked what sorts of things, she responded, "My daddy took me fishing last week. I don't know if I like fishing, but I like being with Daddy. Mom and I went to the zoo the day after my birthday. My favorite place was the monkey house. We watched one eat a banana. It was fun."

Jared is twelve. "I know my dad loves me because he spends time with me. We do lots of things together. He has season tickets to the Wake Forest football games and we never miss a game. I know my mom loves me too, but we don't spend much time together because she often doesn't feel well."

Ten-year-old Brandon said, "My mom loves me. She comes to my soccer games and we go out to eat afterward. I don't know if my dad loves me. He said he did, but he left us. I don't ever see him."

Haley, sixteen, said, "How do I know my parents love me? Mainly because they are always there for me. I can discuss anything with them. I know that they will be understanding and try to help me make good decisions. I'm going to miss them when I go to college in a couple of years, but I know they'll still be there for me."

For those children who crave time with their parents, and for all the others as well, a parent's gift of focused attention is an essential element in ensuring that they feel loved. When you spend time with your children, you are creating memories that will last a lifetime. You want your children to be blessed by the memories they carry from the years they spend in your home. They will have healthy and uplifting memories when their emotional tanks are kept full. As parents, you can give such healthy and uplifting memories and help assure your children's balance, stability, and happiness for the rest of their lives.

IF YOUR CHILD'S LOVE LANGUAGE IS
QUALITY TIME:

Here are a few more ideas especially for parents. Pick and choose among them to try something new you think your child will appreciate.

- Instead of waiting until all your chores are done before spending time with your child, include them in your daily activities such as laundry, grocery shopping, or yard work. Though it may take longer, the time together will make up for the inconvenience.

- Stop what you are doing to make eye contact with your child as they tell you something important.

- Fix a healthy snack together, such as a plate of cut-up fruit.

- Find silly things to laugh about and laugh a lot about them.

- Give older children single-use cameras to record meaningful occasions.

- Turn off your television show to watch your child's favorite show with them.

- Go to the toy store and play with some fun toys with no intention of buying anything.

- Ask very specific questions about your child's day that do not have a yes or no answer.

- When taking your younger children to a park or playground, spend the time actually playing with them instead of watching from the park bench. Pushing your daughter on the swing or riding the slide with your son creates lifelong memories and communicates love.

- Instead of screen time, focus on arts such as singing together or finger painting.

- Schedule a specific "date time" with each of your children individually. Put it in your calendar and don't allow other priorities to take its place.

- Surprise your child with tickets or a trip to a special place. A camping trip, big-league baseball game, or day in the city can build lifelong memories. Add pictures of the event to further strengthen this surprise.

- If possible, take your child to your workplace one day. Introduce your child to your coworkers and take your child to lunch with you.

- Set aside a special place in the house where you go to play. A walk-in closet can serve as a "castle," while a place in the garage can serve as your "workshop."

- Involve older children in vacation planning, researching the Internet together.

- Have a campout together, even if it is simply a tent in your yard. Include flashlights and special camp foods to make the event complete.

- Occasionally take family walks or bike rides together. Seek opportunities to spend time together that also include exercise.

- Share more meals together as a family. Make dinnertime a special occasion with lots of talk about the day. Family prayer can also strengthen this time.

- Spend a few extra minutes putting your child to bed at night. Bedtime stories, talking about the day, or praying together at night can each be part of your everyday pattern.

- For older children, spend time doing "homework" together—they with their schoolwork and you with any work projects. Tell them what you're working on.

- Plant something together. For those with outdoor-oriented children, time together in a flower garden, planting summer vegetables, or landscaping the yard can create lifelong positive memories.

- Make photo albums together on your computer. Talk together about the memories you shared in the process.

- On a rainy day, sit in the same room and read quietly, each of you with your own book or magazine.

GIFTS

5

LOVE LANGUAGE #4:

Gifts

When we asked ten-year-old Rachel why she was so sure that her parents loved her, she said, "Come to my room and I'll show you." Once in her room, she pointed to a large teddy bear. "They brought me this from California." And then touching a fluffy stuffed clown, she said, "They bought me this when I went to first grade. And this silly monkey was from their trip to Hawaii for their anniversary." She continued around the room, pointing out more than a dozen gifts she had received from her parents over the past few years. All of them were in a special place, displaying her parents' love.

The giving and receiving of gifts can be a powerful expression of love, at the time they are given and often extending into later years. The most meaningful gifts become symbols of love, and those that truly convey love are part of a love language. Yet for parents to truly speak love language number four—gifts—the child must feel that his parents genuinely care. For this reason, the other love languages must be given along with a gift. The child's emotional love tank needs to be kept filled in order for the gift to express heartfelt love. This means that parents will use a combination of physical touch, words of affirmation, quality time, and service to keep the love tank full.

Julie told how the love languages were helping her to better understand her two daughters—Mallory, six, and Meredith, eight. "My husband and I often go on business trips and the girls stay with their grandmother. While we are away, I buy something for the girls. Meredith is always much more excited about the gifts than Mallory is, talking about them as soon as we get home. She jumps up and down in excitement as we take out the presents and oohs and ahhs as she opens her gift. Then she finds a special nook in her room for it and wants us to see where she put it. When her friends come over, she always shows them her latest gift."

In contrast, while Mallory is polite and appreciates the gifts from her parents, she is more excited to learn about the trip. Mallory "comes to us to hear every detail of our trip," Julie reported. "She talks with us separately and then together, and seems to drink up everything we tell her. Meredith, on the other hand, asks few questions about where we have been and what we have seen."

When someone asked Julie what she was going to do with her insight, she said, "Well, I'm going to keep on buying gifts for the girls, because I want to. But now I don't feel hurt when Mallory doesn't act as excited as Meredith. It used to bother me because I thought Mallory wasn't being appreciative. Now I understand that our conversation means to Mallory what the gift means to Meredith. Both my husband and I are making more effort to give Mallory more quality time after a trip and all the rest of the year as well. And we want to teach Mallory the language of gifts just as we hope to teach Meredith to speak the language of quality time."

THE GRACE OF GIVING

Giving and receiving gifts as a way to express love is a universal phenomenon. The English word *gift* comes from the Greek word *charis,* which means "grace, or an undeserved gift." The idea behind this is that if the gift is deserved, then it is payment. A true gift is not payment for services rendered; rather, it is an expression of love for the individual and is freely given by the donor. In our society, not all giving is so sincere. Especially in the business world, much of it is payback for doing business with a certain company, or a bribe in hope that someone will do business in the future. The item is not given simply for the benefit of the receiver but is more a way of saying thank you for making a financial contribution or a request for a further contribution.

The same distinction needs to be made in parental giving to children. When a parent offers a gift if the child will clean his room, this is not a true gift but a payment for services rendered. When a parent promises an ice cream cone to a child if he will watch TV for the next half hour, the cone is not a gift but a bribe designed to manipulate the child's behavior. While the child may not know the words *payback* or *bribe*, he understands the concept.

At times parents who have every intention of offering a true gift may be sending confused messages if they ignore the child's deep emotional need for love. In fact, a child who doesn't feel truly loved can easily misinterpret a gift, thinking it is conditionally given. One mother, under great stress and at odds with her son, gave him a new baseball. Later, she found it in the toilet.

"Jason, what's your ball doing here? Don't you like it?"

"Sorry," was Jason's only reply.

The next day she found the ball in the garbage can. Again she talked with him, and he just looked down and said, "I'm sorry."

Later Mom learned to concentrate on keeping Jason's emotional tank full, especially at bedtime. Soon she began to notice a change. In a few weeks, she gave him a baseball bat, and this time he hugged her and said with a smile, "Thanks, Mom!"

Jason is typical of compliant children who have empty emotional tanks. These children seldom show their pain and their needs openly but display their feelings in indirect ways. The disposing or ignoring of gifts is a classic example of this type of child needing a fill-up.

MAKE THE MOST OF GIVING

The grace of giving has little to do with the size and cost of the gift. It has everything to do with love. Maybe you remember a grandparent who told you about receiving an orange plus a necessary item of clothing on one harsh Christmas during the Depression. Today we parents don't always think of necessities as gifts but as items we must supply for our children. And yet, we often give these items with loving hearts for the sincere benefit of our children. Let's celebrate such gifts. If we do not present gifts as expressions of love, children may learn to receive them as "what is to be expected" and not recognize the love behind the gifts.

Here's a suggestion to help a common gift become an expression of love. Take time to wrap up the new school clothes and then present them when the family is gathered around the dinner table. Unwrapping a present provides an emotional thrill for a child, and you can demonstrate that every gift, whether a necessity or a luxury, is an expression of your love. Such celebration of all kinds of gifts will also teach your children how to respond to others who give them presents. As you give to them with grace, you want them to respond with grace, whether a gift is large or small.

One warning in buying your children toys as gifts: in the toy department, you need real wisdom. The sheer volume of items available means that you must be very selective. This volume is compounded by television ads that parade the latest toys before the eyes of children, thus creating desires that did not exist sixty seconds before and may be gone by the next day. But in the meantime, many children are sure they must have the toy they just saw on the screen.

Do not let advertisers determine what you buy for your children. Examine toys closely, asking yourself questions such as, "What message does this toy communicate to my child? Is it a message with which I am comfortable? What might my child learn from playing with this toy? Will its overall effect tend to be positive or negative? How durable is the toy? What is its normal life span? Does it have limited appeal or will my child turn to it again and again? Is this a toy we can afford?" Never buy a nonessential toy if you can't afford it.

Not every toy needs to be educational, but they should all serve some positive purpose in the life of your children. Beware of buying high-tech computerized toys that may expose your children to value systems far removed from those of your family. They will get enough of this on television, from the neighbors, and from friends at school.

WHEN GIVING IS ABUSED

Be careful. It's often tempting to shower children with gifts as substitutes for the other love languages. For many reasons, parents sometimes resort to presents rather than being truly present to their children. For some who grew up in unhealthy families, a gift seems easier to give than emotional involvement. Others may not have the time, patience, or knowledge to know how to give their children what they genuinely need. They truly love their children, but seem unaware of how to provide the emotional security and sense of self-worth that they need.

Abuse of gift-giving can occur when a child is living with a custodial parent following a separation or divorce. The noncustodial parent is often tempted to shower a child with gifts, perhaps from the pain of separation or feelings of guilt over leaving the family. When these gifts are overly expensive, ill-chosen, and used as a comparison with what the custodial parent can provide, they are really a form of bribery, an attempt to buy the child's love. They may also be a subconscious way of getting back at the custodial parent.

Children receiving such ill-advised gifts may eventually see them for what they are, but in the meantime they are learning that at least one parent regards gifts as a substitute for genuine love. This can make children materialistic and manipulative, as they learn to manage people's feelings and behavior by the improper use of gifts. This kind of substitution can have tragic consequences for the children's character and integrity.

We think of Danielle, who is raising three children alone. Danielle had been divorced for three years from Charles, who now lives with his second wife in a luxurious lifestyle. Danielle and the children were just getting by financially, and the children were eager to visit Dad. Lisa, Charley, and Annie, ages fifteen, twelve, and ten, saw their dad two weekends a month. On these visits he would take them on expensive outings such as skiing and boating. No wonder they wanted to visit—that's where the fun was—and they increasingly complained about being bored at home. They often returned with lavish gifts, and they displayed increasing amounts of anger at Danielle, especially for the few days following a visit with their father. Charles was turning their feelings against their mom, as he tried to earn affection for himself. He didn't realize that as the children grew older, they would come to despise him for manipulating them.

Fortunately, Danielle was able to persuade Charles to receive counseling with her and to seek healthy ways to handle their children. Initially, this meant setting aside past differences and anger so that they could work together to meet the emotional needs of their children. During the counseling, they both became expert love tank filler-uppers. When Charles used all five love languages to relate to his children, and learned to use gift-giving as a love language instead of a manipulating device, the children responded beautifully.

> **Appropriate toys should help a child learn how to focus his attention with enjoyment.**

Other parents (and grandparents) may choose to shower their kids with so many presents that their rooms look like disorganized toy stores. With such excess, the gifts lose their specialness; the child has more toys than he can possibly experience. Eventually none of the gifts has any meaning, and the child becomes emotionally dead to receiving gifts. The toys seem a burden to him, because his parents expect him to keep the toys in some semblance of order.

Lavishing too many gifts is like taking a child into the toy department and saying, "All of this belongs to you." The child may be excited at first, but after a while is running in all directions and playing with nothing.

Appropriate toys should help a child learn how to focus his attention with enjoyment. For this to happen, parents and grandparents may need to give less rather than more, carefully choosing gifts that will be meaningful rather than impressive.

GUIDELINES FOR GIVING

As you give to your children, you need to keep some guidelines in mind. Gifts should be genuine expressions of love. If they are payment for services rendered, or bribery, you should not call them gifts but should acknowledge them for what they are. This way, the true gifts selected for the benefit of your children and as an expression of love can be enjoyed for what they are.

Except for Christmas and birthdays, many gifts should be chosen by both you and your children. This is particularly true as your children grow and have more opinions about their clothes, shoes, backpacks, etc. Your children also have desires about their nonessential toys, and while you can't give them everything they want, you will want to consider their preferences. This involves discerning whether the desire is momentary or lasting, healthy or unhealthy, and whether the toy will have a positive or negative effect. Whenever you can, it is wise to select a gift that a child truly wants.

And remember, not all gifts come from a store. You may find a special gift as you walk down a winding road or even across a parking lot. Wildflowers, unusual stones, even driftwood can qualify as gifts when wrapped or presented in a creative manner. Gifts can also be made out of household items. Young children have no concept of money, and whether a gift is made or purchased is of little consequence. If the present stimulates their creativity, it can be meaningful and can bind you more closely to your children in love.

AMY'S RING

Earlier we said that some children who do not respond with great enthusiasm when they receive a gift may in later years come to value it much more. Ted found that out years after his daughter rejected his present. While traveling abroad, Ted bought a ring for his twelve-year-old daughter, Amy, and gave it to her when he returned home. She showed little interest in it and put it away in a dresser drawer.

Ted was disappointed but eventually forgot about the ring. In her teen years, Amy gave her parents great amounts of grief with her adolescent behavior, to the point that Ted despaired about her future. Even when Amy made a dramatic recovery in her attitudes and behavior, her father was still not convinced that she was all right. He questioned her sincerity and this made it very difficult for either of them to move toward the close relationship they craved.

Then one day Ted noticed that Amy was wearing the ring he had given her so long ago, before her problems began. Tears came to his eyes as he realized what his daughter was trying to tell him—that she was in control of herself and could now be trusted.

When Ted asked Amy if this is what she meant, she acknowledged that was all she wanted—to be trusted as she developed and changed. The two cried together. Amy continues to do well.

This story shows how symbolically important a gift can be. Amy probably would have never had the deep problems she experienced if her caring parents had been able to keep her emotional tank full. Her emotional needs had to be met before she had the capacity to receive or appreciate a gift in the same spirit in which it was given.

WHEN YOUR CHILD'S PRIMARY LOVE LANGUAGE IS RECEIVING GIFTS

Most children respond positively to gifts, but for some, receiving gifts is their primary love language. You might be inclined to think that this is so for all children, judging from the way they beg for things. It is true that all children—and adults—want to have more and more. But those whose language of love is receiving gifts will respond differently when they get their gift.

Children whose primary love language is the receiving of gifts will always make much of receiving the gift. They will want the present to be wrapped or at least given in a unique and creative way. This is all part of the love expression. They will look at the paper, maybe talk about the bow. Often they will ooh and aah as they open the gift. It will seem a big deal to them—and it is. They are feeling very special as they open the present, and they want your undivided attention as they do so. Remember, for them this is love's loudest voice. They see the gift as an extension of you and your love, and they want to share this moment with you. Once they have opened the gift, they will hug you or thank you profusely.

These children will also make a special place in their room for the new gift so that they can display it proudly. They will share it with their friends and will show it to you again and again in the next few days. They will say how much they like it. The gift holds a special place in their hearts because it is in fact an expression of your love. Seeing the gift reminds them that they are loved. It doesn't matter to them if the gift was made, found, or purchased; whether it was something they had desired or not. What matters is that you thought about them.

WHAT THE CHILDREN SAY

The comments from the following children reveal that, for them, receiving gifts is the language that best communicates love.

Marco, five, was talking to his grandmother after his second day in kindergarten. "My teacher loves me, Nana. Look what she gave me." He held up a bright blue ruler with large numbers printed across it, the evidence of his teacher's love.

Elizabeth, six, asked us: "Have you ever met the love man? He is right over there," she said, pointing to an older gentleman. "He gives all the children gum." For Elizabeth, he was the love man because he gave gifts.

Courtney, fifteen, was asked how she knew her parents loved her. Without hesitation she pointed to her jeans, top, and shoes. Then she said, "Everything I have, they gave me. In my mind, that's love. They have given me not only the essentials but far more than I need. In fact, I share things with my friends whose parents can't afford them."

Josh, eighteen, was leaving for college in a few weeks. When we asked how strongly he felt loved by his parents, on a zero-to-ten scale, he immediately said, "Ten." Why ten? "See this car?" he asked, pointing to a red Honda. "My folks gave it to me. I didn't really deserve it because I didn't do my best in high school, but they told me they wanted me to know that they were proud of me. This car was an expression of their love. All I have to do is be responsible for changing the oil and doing other maintenance.

"My parents have always been like that. They have given me everything I have ever needed—all my sports equipment in high school, all my clothes, everything. They are the most generous people I know. I have tried not to take advantage of their generosity, but I'm sure that they love me. Now that I'm going off to college, I know that I will miss them."

For such a child, gifts are more than material objects. They are tangible expressions of love that speak deeply. That is why it is especially traumatic if the gifts are destroyed or misplaced. And, if the parent who gave the gift moves or damages it or, in a fit of rage, says, "I'm sorry I gave that to you," the child may be emotionally devastated.

Remember, your children may not now realize how much you are giving, even as you continue to fill their emotional tanks. But as they grow older, they may look back and realize that your love and presence has been the best gift of all.

IF YOUR CHILD'S LOVE LANGUAGE IS
GIFTS:

Here are a few more ideas especially for parents. Pick and choose among them to try something new you think your child will appreciate.

- Keep a small collection of inexpensive gifts packed away for your child. Then give them one at a time as you sense there is a need.

- Select presents that fit the interests of your child.

- Carry snacks or small candies you can give out as a "treat" when away from home.

- Make a meal you know your child likes, go to a special restaurant, or make their favorite dessert.

- Start a collection of unique gift boxes and wrapping papers that can be used to package even the most simple of presents.

- When away from home, mail a small package to your child with their name on it.

- Give personally made coupons for your child, good for some of their favorites, such as a free spaghetti dinner, an extra-half hour of time with you before bedtime, or a small gift next time you are shopping together.

- Keep a "gift bag" of small, inexpensive gifts your child can choose from as a reward for doing something positive.

- Make after-school snacks memorable by serving them on a special plate or making a "face" out of grapes and baby carrots.

- Be on the lookout for personalized gifts with your child's name on them. Save them for a rainy or difficult day as an encouraging surprise.

- Give your child a "song," either one you make up or a special song you select that reminds you of them.

- Create a treasure hunt for a gift that includes a map and clues along the way to the main surprise.

- Hide a small gift in your child's lunchbox.

- If you are away from your child a few days, leave a small package for each day with a special gift and note reminding how much you love them.

- Instead of spending money on a larger gift for a birthday, host a birthday party at a special event location.

- Consider a gift that lasts, such as a tree you can plant together or a computer game you can play together in the future.

- Buy or make your child a special ring or necklace to wear that is just from you.

- For young children, find "nature gifts" such as wildflowers or interesting stones wrapped in a special paper or box.

- For a birthday or Christmas, shop with your child for a special gift—asking her opinion. This personal involvement will make the gift more meaningful.

- Keep a chart and some fun stickers to keep a record of accomplishments. Reward your child with a gift after a set number of stickers are earned.

- Create a "secret drawer" where your child can keep her small "treasures"—anything from a bird feather to a pack of gum.

ACTS OF SERVICE

6

L O V E L A N G U A G E #5:

Acts of Service

Jacob has just started his first full-time job and is thinking about getting married next summer. He also is remembering his childhood: "I think the thing that made me feel most loved was the way my parents worked so hard to help me with everything. I remember how they'd get up early on Saturdays to take me to my games, or stay up late helping me with a homework project."

The twenty-four-year-old continues to reminisce. "The little things and big things—they did so much to help me, even though they were both busy. I realize it now more than I did then, but even at the time I knew they were working hard to help me, and I always appreciated it. I hope I can do the same for my children someday."

Some people speak acts of service as their primary love language. Even if your child does not, know this: parenting is a service-oriented vocation. The day you found out that you would have a child, you enrolled for full-time service. Your contract called for a minimum of eighteen years of service with an understanding that you would be on "active reserve" for several years after that.

As a parent who must serve, you probably have discovered another truth about this love language: Acts of service are physically and emotionally demanding. Therefore, we parents must give attention to our own physical and emotional health. For physical health, we need balanced patterns of sleeping, eating, and exercising. For emotional health, self-understanding and a mutually supportive marital relationship are crucial.

As we consider acts of service, we must ask ourselves, "Who do I serve?" It is not just your children. If you are married, you serve your spouse, doing things that will please him or her in order to express your love. You want to keep your partner's love tank full by your acts of service. Because children need a mother and father who give them a balanced model for life, making time for your marital relationship is an essential part of good parenting. If you are a single parent, it is even more important to keep yourself physically and emotionally healthy—see "Speaking the Love Languages in Single-Parent Families" on page 177 for some ideas.

WHAT'S BEST?

As parents, we serve our children—but our primary motivation is not to please them. Our chief purpose is to do what is best. What would most please your children at the moment is likely not the best way to express your love. Put three candy bars in your child's lunch and she will cheer, but you won't be giving her what's best. In serving your children, the main motive—doing what's best—means you are trying to fill their love tanks. And to supply that need for love, you should use your acts of service in conjunction with the other languages of love.

A caution as we explore the final love language: Don't view acts of service as a way to manipulate your children. This is easy to do, because when they are young, children desire gifts and services more than anything else. But if we parents give in to desires or even demands for too many gifts and too much service, our children can remain childishly self-centered and become selfish. However, this caution should not keep parents from using the language of service and gifts in appropriate ways.

> We serve our children; but as they are ready, we teach them how to serve themselves and then others.

Acts of service can become a model for your child's service and responsibility. You may wonder how your children will develop their own independence and competence if you serve them. But as you express your love by acts of service to your children, doing things they may not yet be able to do for themselves, you are setting a model. This will help them escape their self-centered focus and help others. That's our ultimate goal as parents (see the section "The Ultimate Purpose of Service" on page 98).

WHAT A CHILD SHOULD DO WHEN

Children with full love tanks are far more likely to pick up on that loving model of service than children who are uncertain of their parents' love. Such acts of service must be age appropriate. You should do for your children what they cannot do for themselves. Obviously, you are not still feeding them when they are six. Making beds for four-year-olds is an act of service, but eight-year-olds are capable of doing this themselves. Children don't need to wait until they get to college to learn how to run a washer and dryer—colleges don't offer courses in this! Parents who are too busy to teach children how to do laundry, or too perfectionistic to let them do it, are not loving those children but crippling them.

Thus, acts of service have an intermediate step. We serve our children; but as they are ready, we teach them how to serve themselves and then others. Of course, that is not always a convenient or quick process. It takes more time to teach a child to prepare a meal than to fix the meal yourself. If your only objective is to get the food on the table, you might as well prepare all the meals. But if your objective is to love your children—looking out for their best interests—you will want to teach them how to cook. But before and during that time, the best motivator for your children is to see your genuine acts of love for the family as you serve them over many years.

Remember, too, that some acts of service you will perform for your children come from highly developed skills you have that they may never acquire. We all have different aptitudes, and within a family we can serve one another with our unique abilities. As parents we must be careful not to force children to be replicas of us or, even worse, fulfill the dreams we never accomplished for ourselves. Rather, we want to help them develop their own skills, follow their own interests, and become the best they can be using their endowments from God.

SHOOTIN' STRAIGHT

Some parents, wanting their children to develop their skills and independence, lean too far in the direction of letting their children figure things out for themselves. Will and Kathy from Colorado were like that. They embodied a pioneer spirit of rugged independence and self-reliance and wanted to raise their two boys to be the same way. Western to the core, they seemed as if they had just swung off a stagecoach.

After Will and Kathy attended my (Gary's) marriage seminar and heard about the five love languages, they concluded that service could not be one of the languages of love. Will told me, "I don't believe parents should do things for children that they can do for themselves. How are you gonna teach them to be independent if you keep on doing things for them? They've got to learn to rope their own steer."

"Do the boys cook their own meals?" I asked.

"That's my job. But they do everything else," Kathy said.

"They cook when they are out on the trail and do a great job," Will added. These two were obviously proud of their sons.

"As you listened to the love languages, do you have any idea what your boys' primary love languages might be?"

"Don't know," Will said.

"Do you think your boys really feel loved?"

"Suppose so. They should."

"Do you have the courage to ask them?" I probed.

"What do you mean?"

"I mean, get each of them alone and say, 'Son, I want to ask you a question that I've never asked you, but it is important for me to know. Do you feel that I love you? Shoot straight. I really want to know how you feel.'"

Will was silent for a long moment. "That'll be hard. Don't know that it's necessary."

"It's not necessary," I responded, "but you won't ever know their language if you don't ask."

Will went home with my words ringing in his head, "You won't ever know if you don't ask." So he started with his younger son, Buck, out behind the barn when they were alone. He asked the question I had suggested and Buck answered.

"Sure, Dad, I know you love me. You spend time with me. When you go into town, you always take me along. On the trail, you make sure we get some time to talk. I've always thought it was pretty special to get to spend so much time with you, as busy as you are." When Will choked up, Buck asked, "Is something wrong? You ain't gonna die or something, are ya?"

"Naw, I ain't gonna die. I just wanted to make sure you know I love you."

This was such an emotional experience that it took Will a week to work up the courage to talk with seventeen-year-old Jake. One night when they were alone together after supper, he turned to his son and said, "Jake, I want to ask you a question that I've never asked before, but it's important for me to know. It might be hard for you, but I want you to shoot straight, because I really need to know how you feel. Do you really feel that I love you?"

After a long silence, Jake said, "I don't know how to say this exactly, Pa. I guess I know you love me, but sometimes I don't feel it. Sometimes I feel that you don't love me at all."

"When's that, Son?"

"When I need you and you don't help me. Like the time the fire started on the lower forty and I sent word by Buck that I needed your help. He came back and told me that you said you knew I could do it by myself. Buck and I got it out all right, but I kept wondering why you didn't come. I kept telling myself that it was 'cause you were trying to make me independent, but I kept feeling you didn't love me.

"That time when I was ten and having a hard time with my math, I asked you to help," Jake continued. "You told me I could do it myself 'cause I was smart. I knew you knew how to do it, and you could have helped me if you would have just explained it. I felt let down. Or that time the wagon got stuck and I asked you to help me get it out. You said I got it stuck and I could figure out how to get it out. I knew I could get it out, but I wanted you to help me.

"Them's the times I felt you didn't care. Like I said, I know you do love me, but I don't always feel that you do."

It was enough to make a cowboy cry. "Jake, I'm sorry," Will said. "I just didn't know how you felt. I should've asked you sooner. I wanted you to be independent and self-reliant—and you are. I'm proud of you, but I want you to know that I love you. The next time you need my help, I'll be there for you. I hope you give me another chance." The two men hugged in the quiet kitchen.

Will got his chance about seven months later when a wagon was stuck in the creek. The boys worked more than two hours and couldn't loosen it. Finally, Jake sent Buck for their dad. Buck couldn't believe his father's response when he immediately saddled up and rode back with Buck to the creek. Once the wagon was out, Buck thought it strange that his dad hugged Jake and then told Jake, "Thanks, man. I appreciate it." The healing that started in the kitchen was consummated at the creek. A tough rancher had learned a tender lesson.

LOVING SERVICE OR LIFETIME LABOR?

Because service to a child is constant for so many years, and takes place in and around so many other obligations, parents can forget that the daily and mundane acts they perform are expressions of love with long-term effects. At times they can even feel more like unpaid laborers than loving servants, put upon by spouse, children, and others. However, if they assume this attitude, it will communicate itself emotionally to the child, who will feel that he is receiving little love from the acts of service.

Loving service is not labor, as some fear. Labor is usually imposed from the outside and is done with reluctance. Loving service is an internally motivated desire to give one's energy to others. Loving service is a gift, not a necessity, and is done freely, not under coercion. When parents serve their children with a spirit of resentment and bitterness, a child's physical needs may be met, but his emotional development will be greatly hampered.

Because service is so daily, even the best parents need to stop for an attitude check now and then, to be sure that their acts of service are communicating love.

THE ULTIMATE PURPOSE OF SERVICE

The ultimate purpose for acts of service to children is to help them emerge as mature adults who are able to give love to others through acts of service. This includes not only being helpful to cherished loved ones but also serving persons who are in no way able to return or repay the kindnesses. As children live with the example of parents who serve the family and those beyond the walls of their home, they too will learn to serve.

It is difficult for children to feel good about expressing appreciation when they are commanded to do so.

The Bible suggests that sacrificial service is one way we please God. While dining in the home of a prominent religious leader, Jesus told His host:

When you give a luncheon or dinner, do not invite your friends, your brothers or sisters, your relatives, or your rich neighbors; if you do, they may invite you back and so you will be repaid. But when you give a banquet, invite the poor, the crippled, the lame, the blind, and you will be blessed.[1]

What powerful words! This is what we want for our children—to be able to perform acts of service with compassion and genuine love.

But our children are immature. They are naturally self-centered and cannot be expected to serve others with selfless motivation. They want to be rewarded for their good behavior. It takes a long time for them to be able to give love through selfless acts of service.

How do we move toward this ultimate goal? First, we make sure that our children feel genuinely loved and cared for. We keep their emotional tanks full. Also, we are role models for them. By our example, they first experience loving acts of service. As they grow older and are able to show appreciation, we can gradually move from commands to requests. Requests do not demand. It is difficult for children to feel good about expressing appreciation when they are commanded to do so. It is the difference between "Say thank you to your father," or "Would you say thank you to your father?" Making requests is more soothing, forestalls anger, and helps us be positive and pleasant.

As children mature, they increasingly notice what is being done for them and are also aware of what has been done in the past. Of course, they don't remember anyone changing their diapers or feeding them. But they see other parents caring for their infants in this way and know that they enjoyed the same acts of service. With an assurance of being genuinely loved, they are able to appreciate when food is prepared and served. They will become more aware of story times and family play, of parents teaching them to ride a bicycle, helping them with homework, caring for them when they are ill, comforting their feelings when they are hurt, taking them to special places, and buying treats and gifts.

Eventually these children will notice that their parents do things for others. They will learn how to wait on a sick person or to give money to the less fortunate. They will want to participate in work projects that help other people, especially those adventures that take them out of their familiar routine. They don't have to travel far to find the less fortunate. In most towns of any size, there are people in need. Your family, either alone or with a community or church group, can take a day or a week to offer your services to a mission, a camp for underprivileged children, a food pantry or soup kitchen, a mission, or a nursing home. When parents and their children work together in such acts of service, the activity becomes a powerful lesson in the joys of helping others.

And, of course, there are those occasional more exotic service opportunities overseas through work or private organizations. One year I (Ross) volunteered as a doctor with a Christian mission agency—Wycliffe Bible Translators—in Bolivia. The whole Campbell family came and helped. I remember treating a three-year-old Indian boy with a badly broken leg in our clinic. For six weeks he was in traction and unable to be moved. Many missionary children there performed acts of service for the little boy. I was thrilled at Christmas, when our Carey, then eight years old, gave the boy's sister her most treasured Christmas gift, a new doll.

TEACHING BY EXAMPLE

The heart of social and missionary service is a desire to help others with acts of service. Yet parents can get off track and actually prevent their children from being able to give of themselves unselfishly. We must be careful in our acts of service to never show conditional love. When parents give of themselves to their children only when they are pleased by their behavior, such acts of service are conditional. Our watching children will learn that a person should help others only if there is something in it for him.

"What's in it for me?" is a predominant attitude in our society. And yet, it is exactly opposite to the love language of acts of service (and contrary to the heart of Christian social and missionary service). You may be one of the children raised in this self-involved mindset. Now you want your own children to develop into people of integrity. You want them to be kind and generous to others, particularly to the less fortunate, without expecting anything in return. And you may wonder if that is possible in our society.

It certainly is possible, but it depends very much on you. Your children need to see in you the traits you want them to develop. They need to experience your acts of service to them and be involved in your caring for other people. You can teach them by example to show concern for others.

"DO-GOOD PROJECTS"

One of the finest ways to do this is by hosting others in your home. Family hospitality is a great treasure, for in this act of service, people truly get to know each other and to form strong friendships. As you open your home to others, your children learn this meaningful way of sharing love with friends and family.

In the Chapman family, we had an open house every Friday night for college students when our kids were young. The students came from nearby schools, including Wake Forest University, and we'd pack in from twenty to sixty students. Our format was simple. From 8 to 10 p.m. we had a discussion about a relational, moral, or social issue, drawn from a Bible passage. Next came refreshments followed by informal conversations. At midnight we kicked them out.

Our children, Shelley and Derek, wandered in and out of the meetings. It was not unusual to find one of them sleeping in a student's lap by the fireplace, or engaging someone in conversation. The students were our extended family, and the children looked forward to Friday evenings.

Often on Saturday mornings, some of the students returned for what we came to call "Do-Good Projects." We would load up in the van and distribute them around the community to rake leaves for the elderly or clean gutters or other jobs that needed to be done. Shelley and Derek always went along on these service projects. And yes, they insisted on having their own rakes, although their greatest joy was to jump in the leaves after they were raked.

As adults, Shelley and Derek look back on this involvement with students as a significant part of their childhood. Shelley, who is now an OB/GYN physician, acknowledges that talking with the students from Bowman Gray Medical School made a strong impression on her choice of vocation. Both she and Derek are very people-oriented. Derek has been known to invite street people into his apartment during the winter (did we really teach him this?). We are convinced that sharing our home with others and involving the family in service projects had a profound and positive effect on our children.

Make it your goal that your children will learn to be comfortable in serving others. Your children won't pick this up by accident. Rather, they will learn it as they watch you serving them and other people. They will also learn as you give them small levels of responsibility for helping you serve. As they grow, you can increase what they do.

WHEN YOUR CHILD'S PRIMARY LOVE LANGUAGE IS SERVICE

Acts of service that are genuine expressions of love will communicate on an emotional level to most children. However, if service is your child's primary love language, your acts of service will communicate most deeply that you love Johnny or Julie. When that child asks you to fix a bicycle or mend a doll's dress, he or she does not merely want to get a task done; your child is crying for emotional love. That's what Jake was really asking his dad, Will, to do.

When we parents recognize and respond to these requests and give the help with a loving and positive attitude, the child will go away with a full love tank, as Jake did. But when parents refuse to respond to the needs, or do so with harsh or critical words, the child may ride off on a repaired bike, but do so with a discouraged spirit.

If your child's primary love language is acts of service, this does not mean that you must jump at every request. It does mean that you should be extremely sensitive to those requests and recognize that your response will either help fill the child's love tank or else puncture the tank. Each request calls for a thoughtful, loving response.

WHAT THE CHILDREN SAY

Look at what the following children say about their primary love language.

Isabella, age seven, has had numerous health problems during the past three years. "I know Mommy loves me 'cause when I need help with my homework, she helps me. When I have to go to the doctor, she gets off from work and takes me. When I am really sick, she fixes my favorite soup."

Bradley, twelve, lives with his mother and younger brother. His father left when Bradley was six. "I know my mom loves me because she sews the buttons on my shirt when they fall off and also helps me with my homework every night. She works hard in an office so we can have food and clothes. I think my dad loves me, but he doesn't do much to help."

Jodi, fourteen, attends a special education class at the public school. She lives with her mother. "I know Mom loves me because she helps me make my bed and wash my clothes. At night, she helps me do my homework, especially my art."

Melania, also fourteen, is the oldest of four children. "I know my parents love me because they do so many things for me. Mom made my costume for the school drama; in fact, she made costumes for two other people too. That made me really proud of her. Dad has always helped me with my homework, and this year he has really put in some time on my algebra. I couldn't believe he could remember all that stuff."

For these children, their parents' acts of service came through as emotional love. Parents whose children speak this primary love language learn that serving is loving. Serve your child—and others—and they will know you love them.

Here are a few more ideas especially for parents. Pick and choose among them to try something new you think your child will appreciate.

- Help your child practice for their sports team, such as pitch and catch for baseball or shooting free throws for children participating in basketball.

- Sit down and help your child if they're having computer problems.

- Instead of just telling your younger children to go to bed, pick them up and gently carry them and tuck them in their blankets.

- For school-age children, help them select their outfit for the day as they are waking up in the morning.

- Occasionally wake up a half-hour earlier to make a special surprise breakfast for your children.

- Begin teaching your child the importance of serving others through regular involvement together in a local community group or church ministry.

- For younger children, set up your child's favorite toys while they are taking a nap or are at school so they can immediately play with them (with you!).

- When running late to an appointment or meeting, help your child quickly finish what they are doing so you can both be ready faster instead of just telling them to hurry.

- During a time when your child is sick, go the extra step by setting up their favorite movie, reading them stories, or buying them a book in one of their favorite series.

- Connect your child with one of your friends or family members who can help them in an area of interest such as computer technology, soccer, piano playing, or scouting.

- Choose one area in which you determine to always serve your child above and beyond normal expectations. Examples could include making sure there are always marshmallows in your child's hot chocolate, making sure their favorite teddy bear is in their bed at bedtime, or having all of the paint supplies ready when they are ready to paint.

- Start a "birthday dinner" tradition where you make your child any meal they want on their birthday.

- Make a list of several of your child's favorite things they do with you. Then periodically do one of their favorites when they least expect it.

- Create flash cards for your child's upcoming test or quiz. Work together with your child until they feel confident with the material.

- Assist your child in fixing a favorite broken toy or bicycle. Simply taking the time to repair it communicates love to a child whose love language is acts of service.

7

How to Discover Your Child's Primary Love Language

We have introduced you to each of the five love languages, and you have heard the children describe how a certain love language really speaks to them. Yet you may still wonder, *What's my child's primary love language? I'm not sure I know.* Spotting your child's primary language of love may take time, but there are clues all around. This is our detective chapter, in which we help you discover your child's primary love language.

Before you begin to uncover those clues, however, let's consider one other crucial reason it's worth the search. We have mentioned that speaking your child's primary love language helps her feel loved. When your child feels loved, when her emotional tank is full, she will be more responsive to parental guidance in all areas of her life. She will listen without resentment. But there is an equally grand reason to learn your child's love language—and to speak the other four languages as well. As we speak love in the five languages, all the while specializing in her language of love, we show her how to love others and her own need to learn to speak others' love languages.

THE WAY OF UNSELFISHNESS

The ability to give love and nurture in all the languages will make your children more balanced persons who can function well in society. As they do this, they can speak the love languages to meet their own needs and to be of help to others.

All children are selfish, so they are often unaware of the importance of communicating in ways that are not familiar or comfortable. For example, one child may have a problem sharing—and thus in giving gifts. Another may tend to be a loner and find it difficult to understand the need of gregarious people for quality time. A third child may be so behaviorally oriented that he has difficulty communicating verbally. Very quiet children are often this way. Helping such a child to be more verbal, affirmative, and outgoing is a significant expression of love on the part of the parents. He will be learning the important language of affirming words.

When we as parents learn to speak our children's love language, even though it differs from our own, we are showing them the way of unselfishness, the way of serving others. We are guiding them into an important part of becoming an adult—giving and caring for others. Imagine, for instance, if all our children learned to appreciate love language #5, acts of service. Community associations that go begging for volunteers in city cleanup campaigns would have most streets cared for on the big day; they'd have lots of volunteers for the "welcome neighbor" program. Churches would have a waiting list of people wanting to help with committee work and serve behind the scenes.

IT TAKES TIME

Knowing this, we should agree that speaking the five love languages with our children is important, and learning our children's primary language is crucial. How do we learn their language?

It takes time. With an infant, you must express love in all five languages; that's how he will develop emotionally. And yet, even then you may begin to see clues of your child's preferred language—if you are liberally using all of them. For instance, one child may show little response to his mother's voice while another child may find her voice incredibly soothing. One baby may be calmed by the nearness of another person, while another will seem not to notice very much.

As your child grows, you will begin to see that one of the love languages speaks far more deeply of your love than the others; also, when that one is used negatively, your child feels very hurt. Remember those two truths about the five love languages and you will become more effective in expressing your love and less destructive when you feel angry or frustrated with your child.

Discovering your child's love language is a process; it takes time, especially when your child is young. Young children are just beginning to learn how to receive and express love in the various languages. This means that they will experiment with actions and responses that are satisfying to them. That they engage in a particular response for a period of time does not mean that this is their primary love language. In a few months, they may specialize in another one.

Stages in Loving: Cami's Story

In the Campbell family, we were intrigued by watching our granddaughter, Cami, interact with the elderly persons at the nearby nursing home where her great-grandmother lived. Even when she was two and three years old, Cami loved to draw pictures for the residents and give each of them one. She also would make sure that her great-grandmother received enough cards and presents for her birthday and Christmas, even though her great-grandmother had Alzheimer's and did not really know Cami.

It would have been easy for us to assume that Cami's primary love language was acts of service. However, that would have been a mistake, since she was too young for anyone to have an accurate reading on this. Also, we observed her need for attention from her parents, especially physical touch, eye contact, words of affection, and quality time.

As Cami grew, we enjoyed watching her ways of showing and receiving love, all the while remembering that children go through periods where their primary love language can temporarily change, especially during adolescence. We mention this because we want you to remember that a love language is not set in stone. While you need to look for your child's primary language, you also need to keep in mind that children go through stages in loving, as they do in everything else. They experiment in reaching out, just as they do in their hobbies and academic interests. They may seem to prefer one language for receiving love and another for giving it. You want to make sure you do not "peg" a child when he or she may be changing.

The supreme value of discovering your child's primary love language is that it gives you the most effective means of communicating emotional love. When you perceive that your child is discouraged and feeling distant, and you want to express emotional warmth to her, you will know how to focus your love.

DON'T BE FOOLED!

As you begin to look for a child's primary love language, it is better not to discuss your search with your children, and especially with teenagers. By nature children are self-centered. If they see that the concept of love languages is important to you, they may well use it to manipulate you to satisfy their momentary desires. The desires they express may have little to do with their deep emotional needs.

For example, if a child has been begging you for an iPhone, he may see the love language idea as a way to manipulate you to buy the device. All he has to do is to tell you that his primary language is gifts and that if you really love him, you will buy the iPhone. As a conscientious parent wanting to find his primary language, you are likely to buy the phone before you realize that you have been hoodwinked. Remember, positive parenting does not mean giving your children everything they want.

You can employ the following methods as you seek to discover your child's primary love language.

1. Observe How Your Child Expresses Love to You.

Watch your child; he may well be speaking his own love language. This is particularly true of a young child, who is very likely to express love to you in the language he desires most to receive. If your five- to eight-year-old frequently gives you words of appreciation such as, "Mommy, you're pretty," or "Daddy, thanks for helping me with my homework," or "I love you, Mommy," or "Have a good day, Dad," you can rightly suspect that his primary love language is words of affirmation.

This method is not as effective with fifteen-year-olds, particularly those who are accomplished in manipulation. They may have learned by trial and error that if they say positive words, you are more likely to give in to one of their desires, even if you are not completely convinced that you should. For this reason, this first method is best used for children who are between five and ten years of age.

2. Observe How Your Child Expresses Love to Others.

If your first-grader always wants to take a present to his teacher, this may indicate that his primary love language is receiving gifts. However, be careful that you are not suggesting presents for the teacher. If you are, your child is merely following your lead and the gift is not an expression of love, nor is it a clue to his primary love language.

A child whose language is gifts receives tremendous pleasure from getting presents and wants others to enjoy this same pleasure. He assumes that they will feel what he does when they receive a gift.

3. Listen to What Your Child Requests Most Often.

If your child often asks you to "look what I'm doing," play outside together, or sit and read a story to her, she is requesting quality time. If her requests seem to fit this pattern, she is asking for what she needs most emotionally, namely, your undivided attention. Of course, all children need attention, but for one who receives love most deeply this way, the requests for time together will greatly outnumber all the others.

If your child constantly solicits comments on his work, then his love language may be words of affirmation. Questions such as, "Mom, what do you think of the paper I wrote?" or "Does this outfit look okay?" or "Dad, how did I do in the game?" are all requests for words of affirmation. Again, all children need and want such words and will occasionally ask for them. But if your child's requests tend to focus in this area, this is a strong indication that his love language is words of affirmation.

4. Notice What Your Child Most Frequently Complains About.

This approach is related to the third, but, instead of directly asking for something, this time your child is complaining that he is not receiving something from you. If he complains, "You're always busy," or "You always have to take care of the baby," or "We never go to the store together," he is probably revealing more than a simple frustration at the coming of a new baby. He is expressing that since the baby arrived, he is feeling less love from you. In his complaints, he is clearly requesting quality time.

An occasional complaint about the lack of quality time does not indicate the child's primary love language. For example, "Daddy, you work too much" may repeat what a child has heard the mother say. Or, "I wish our family took vacations like Ben's family" may express a desire to be like Ben.

Every child complains now and then. Many of these complaints are related to immediate desires and are not necessarily an indication of a love language. But if the complaints fall into a pattern so that more than half the complaints focus on one love language, then they are highly indicative. Their frequency is the key.

5. Give Your Child a Choice between Two Options.

Lead your child to make choices between two love languages. For example, a father might say to a ten-year-old, "Jamal, I'm going to get off early Thursday afternoon. We could go to the gym together or I could help you pick out some new basketball shoes. Which would you prefer?" The child has a choice between quality time and a gift. A mother might say to her daughter, "I have some free time this evening. We could take Daisy to the dog park or I could help you study for the test. Which would you prefer?" This obvious choice is between quality time and an act of service.

As you give options for several weeks, keep a record of your child's choices. If most of them tend to cluster around one of the five love languages, you have likely discovered which one makes your child feel most loved. At times, your child will not want either option and will suggest something else. You should keep a record of those requests also, since they may give you clues.

If your child wonders what you are up to, giving such choices so frequently, and asks what is going on, you might say, "I've been thinking about how I invest my time with the family. When we have time together, I thought it would be good if I knew your thoughts and feelings about what we do with that time. It has been helpful for me. What do you think?" You can be as philosophical or as simple as you wish. However, what you are saying is true. As you seek to discover your child's love language, you are also giving him an exercise in choice.

USING CHOICES TO DISCOVER THE LOVE LANGUAGE

Choices at Six

The choices you offer your child depend on age and interest. The following are merely examples to stimulate your creativity. To a first-grader you might say:

"Would you like for me to make you some cupcakes *(acts of service)* or for us to have lemonade on the deck *(quality time)*?"

"Would you rather wrestle *(physical touch)* or read a story together *(quality time)*?"

"While I am out of town for two days, would you rather I bring you a present *(gift)* or send you a special email *(words of affirmation)*?"

"Would you like to play our game, 'I like you because . . .' *(words of affirmation)* or would you like me to put up new shelves in your room *(acts of service)?"*

The game, "I like you because . . ." is one in which parent and child take turns completing the sentence, "I like you because . . ." For example, the parent says, "I like you because you have a beautiful smile." Then the child may say, "I like you because you read stories to me." The parent says, "I like you because you are kind to your sister." This is an enjoyable way of giving affirming words to the child and teaching him to affirm the parent. The game may also incorporate the ABCs so that the first "I like you . . ." must start with an A, as in, "Because you are active." The second begins with a B, as in, "Because you are beautiful."

Choices at Ten

If your child is closer to ten years old, you might ask questions such as:

"For your birthday, would you rather have a new bicycle *(gift)* or a trip with me to Washington, DC *(quality time)?"*

"Would you rather I fix your computer this evening *(acts of service)* or that we play basketball together *(quality time* and *physical touch)?"*

"When we see Grandma this weekend, would you prefer that I tell her what a great job you did in school this quarter *(words of affirmation)* or that I buy you a surprise when we are there for doing so well *(gift)?"* You may choose to do both.

"Would you prefer I watch you practice your gymnastics *(quality time)* or that we buy you a new pair of jeans *(gift)?"*

Choices at Fifteen

For a fifteen-year-old, the following choices might be appropriate: You and your child have bought an old car that you are trying to get in good condition by the time he is sixteen. The option is, "This Saturday, would you like us to work on the car together *(quality time)* or would you rather that I work on it while you spend time with your friends *(acts of service)*?"

"Would you prefer we buy you a jacket Saturday afternoon *(gift)* or that the two of us spend time at the cabin while Dad is away *(quality time)*?"

"Since you and I are the only ones at home tonight, would you rather that we eat out *(quality time)* or that I fix your favorite pizza *(acts of service)*?"

"If you were feeling discouraged and I wanted to build you up, which would be more helpful to you—if I sat down and told you how much I love and appreciate you, and then mentioned some of your positive traits *(words of affirmation)* or if I simply gave you a bear hug and said, 'I'm with you, man' *(physical touch)*?"

Giving choices will be helpful only if you do it often enough to see a pattern showing a clear preference in love languages. You will probably need to offer twenty to thirty choices before you can see a clear pattern emerging. Isolated answers may just indicate the preference of the moment.

If you decide to be very creative about this, you could draw up thirty of the either/or choices, being sure that you include an equal number of options for each love language. Then present it to your child as a sort of research project on choices. Most teens will cooperate in such an effort, and the results may give you a clear reading on your child's love language.

A Fifteen-Week Experiment

If none of the above suggestions give you much clue as to your child's primary love language, this one may work for you. But if you begin it, be prepared to continue for the full term, fifteen weeks.

First, choose one of the five love languages to focus on for two weeks, as you express love to your child. For example, if you begin with quality time, each day you will seek to communicate your love by giving your child at least thirty minutes of your undivided attention. One day take her to breakfast. Another day, play a computer word game or read a book together. As you give this amount of undivided attention, observe how your child responds. If, by the end of the two weeks, your child is begging for freedom, you know you have to look elsewhere. If, however, you see a new twinkle in her eye and you are getting positive comments on how much she enjoys your time together, you may have found what you were looking for.

After the two weeks, take a week off, not totally withdrawing but giving about one-third the time you did before. This allows the relationship to move closer to what it was before. Then select another love language and focus on it for the next two weeks. For example, if you choose physical touch, you will touch your child in some meaningful way at least four times every day. So, before he leaves for school, you give him a hug and kiss. When he comes home, you greet him with another quick hug. When he sits down to dinner, rub his back for a minute. Later, when he is doing homework, pat him on the shoulder. Repeat this process every day, varying your expressions of physical touch, but always giving meaningful touches at least four times a day.

Then observe his response. If, by the end of the two weeks, he is pulling back and saying, "Stop touching me," you know this is not his primary love language. But if he is going with the flow, letting you know that it feels good, you may be on the right track.

The following week, draw back somewhat and notice your child's response. Then choose another love language and follow the same scenario. Keep observing your child's behavior as you move through the next weeks. He may begin requesting one language you spoke previously. If so, he is giving you a clue. Or he might complain that you stopped doing what you did two weeks ago; that's a clue too.

If your child wonders what you are up to, you can respond, "I want to love you in every way I can, so that you will know how much I care about you." Don't mention the concept of primary love languages. And, as you are pursuing this experiment, keep in mind that your child still needs love shown through all the love languages— soothing words, focused attention, acts of love, appropriate gifts, and physical touch along with loving eye contact.

If You Have Teenagers . . .

If you are rearing teenagers, you know that this job is like none other in the world. Because of the changes they are experiencing, your teens' giving and receiving of love may also change with their moods. Most teens go through periods that can best be described as "grunt stages," because all you can get out of them is a couple of muffled words that sound like grunts.

Mom: "Hi, honey, how are you doing?"
Tim: "Okay." *(Barely audible)*
Mom: "What have you been up to this morning?"
Tim: "Nuthin'." *(Barely audible)*

A teenager in this difficult stage may not be able to receive any love language except physical touch, and only then if you are quick about it. Of course, these teens do come up for air now and then, and during their more coherent times, you will want to show them all the love you can, particularly in their own primary language.

Teenagers, at times, make it difficult for you to fill their emotional love tank. They are testing you, to see if you really love them. They may do this by acting sullen for no obvious reason, making something more difficult for you than it should be, or simply by being passive-aggressive in their behavior. Such behavior may be their subconscious way of asking, "Do you really love me?"

These behaviors are always a test for parents. If you can remain calm, cool, and kind (firm but kind), you pass the test and your teens will eventually mature beyond that difficult stage.

When Dan was thirteen, he began testing his parents. His father, Jim, felt some initial frustration but then realized that he had let Dan's love tank go dry. Knowing that Dan's primary love language was quality time, he decided to spend a whole weekend with his son, filling that tank up—quite a challenge since teenagers have a large love tank. After their weekend together, Jim felt that he had done what he set out to do, and resolved that he would never again let Dan's love tank run dry.

The evening they came back, Jim had an important meeting, one that Dan knew about. Just as Jim was leaving, Dan called, "Dad, got a minute?" Here was the test. Dan was really asking, "Dad, do you really love me?" So many parents are trapped by this test and blow their cool.

Fortunately, Jim realized what was happening and set a time to talk with Dan. He said, "I have to get to my meeting right now; let's get together as soon as I come home, about 9:30."

If Jim had lost his patience with Dan and said, "I just spent the whole weekend with you! What else do you need?" he could have punctured a hole in the love tank he had just spent forty-eight hours filling.

Becoming Multilingual

Whatever your child's love language may be, remember that it's important to speak all five languages. It is easy to make the mistake of using one love language to the exclusion of the others. This is especially true of gifts, because they seem to take less of our time and energy. But if we fall into the trap of giving our children too many gifts, we deprive them of healthy and full love tanks, and we can also cause them to see the world through materialistic eyes.

In addition, learning to speak all five love languages will help us to nurture people throughout our lives, not only our children but spouses and friends and relatives. Right now, our emphasis is on nurturing our children, but we know that in a few years they will be reaching out to all sorts of people, most of them quite different from themselves.

As parents, we need to remember that learning the love languages is a maturational process, and that becoming mature is a slow, painful, and often difficult journey. As we become multilingual, we also will be helping our children to learn how to give and receive in all the love languages. As we are faithful in loving and providing examples, we can then envision our children moving into their adult lives able to share love with others in so many ways. When this happens, they will be outstanding adults!

8

Discipline and the
Love Languages

Which of the following words is negative: *love, warmth, laughter, discipline*?

The answer is—none. Contrary to what many people think, *discipline* is not a negative word. *Discipline* comes from a Greek word that means "to train." Discipline involves the long and vigilant task of guiding a child from infancy to adulthood. The goal is that the child would reach a level of maturity that will allow him one day to function as a responsible adult in society. Now that's a positive goal!

To train your child in mind and character to become a self-controlled and constructive member of home and community requires that you use every type of communication with the child. You will employ guidance by example, modeling, verbal instruction, written request, teaching and preaching right behavior, correcting wrong behavior, providing learning experiences, and much more. Punishment is also one of these means and does have its place, but in many homes punishment is greatly overused. In fact, many parents assume that discipline and punishment are synonymous. Punishment is a type of discipline, though the most negative.

Some parents, particularly those who did not receive much love in their own childhood, tend to skip the importance of nurturing a child. They regard the main task of parenting as punishment, instead of using other, more positive forms of discipline. To be effective in discipline, parents must keep the child's emotional love tank filled with love. In fact, disciplining without love is like trying to run a machine without oil. It may appear to be working for a while but will end in disaster.

Because of the confusion about discipline, we are focusing in this chapter on the common, corrective meaning of the word, and in the next chapter on the teaching/learning aspects of discipline. In both instances, we will explore how your child's love language can help you to develop discipline in your child.

KEEPING JOHNNY OUT OF THE STREET

The common, popular definition of discipline is the establishing of parental authority, the developing of guidelines for behavior, and then helping children live by these guidelines. Every culture historically has held expectations for mature behavior and has devised means through which this would be achieved.

Historically, all kinds of societies have regarded human beings as moral creatures. Within the larger community, some things are considered right and others wrong; some are acceptable while others are unacceptable. While standards differ from place to place, no society is amoral. Each has its codes, rules, laws, and ethical understandings. When individuals choose to live immoral lives, they do so to their own detriment and to the harm of their society.

Parents play the most important role in the discipline of their children because it is they who interpret to their offspring their culture's generally accepted standards. Babies are not capable of deciding how to live, and without parental rules, a child will not survive to adulthood. During infancy, parents must totally enforce the rules and control the behavior of the child. This means that they will not allow Johnny to crawl into a fire, no matter how attracted he may be to the rising flames. Later, as a toddler, Johnny must be kept out of the street lest he be hit by a passing car. His parents must put medicines and toxic substances out of reach.

From this infantile stage requiring total control, parents move toward devoting more than a decade to rearing their child to an acceptable level of self-discipline. This road to maturity is one that every child must walk and for which every parent needs to accept responsibility. It is an awesome task, requiring wisdom, imagination, patience, and great amounts of love.

Many parents are confused about the "best" way to raise children. They don't trust themselves and are ready to listen to the latest expert. Yet even the experts offer clashing theories and often contradictory advice. This has yielded much disagreement as to the standards for discipline in American families. Thus the patterns of discipline vary greatly in America. It is beyond the scope of this book to deal with the full arena of discipline. If you want to read more about this, you will find suggested books in the appendix.

BEFORE YOU DISCIPLINE

Love looks out for the interests of another; so does discipline. So discipline is certainly an act of love. And the more a child feels loved, the easier it is to discipline that child. The reason is that a child must identify with her parents in order to accept their guidance without resentment, hostility, and obstructive, passive-aggressive behavior. This means that we must keep the child's love tank full before we administer discipline.

If the child does not identify with his parents, he will view each parental request or command as an imposition and will learn to resent it. In extreme cases, the child comes to consider a parental request with such resentment that his total orientation to parental authority—and eventually all authority—becomes one of doing the opposite of what is expected.

Michael is ten years old. His father, Paul, is a lawyer who works long hours. On the weekends, he mows the lawn and does other household jobs. Occasionally he attends a football game on Saturday and often spends time working in his home office. Michael doesn't see much of his father. Since Michael's primary love language is quality time, he doesn't feel much love coming from his dad. By the time the weekend rolls around, his father is physically and emotionally tired—not in a mood to put up with childish pranks.

Practice unconditional love, then discipline.

His discipline is typically accompanied with harsh words said in an angry voice. Paul thinks that his discipline is what his son needs to become a responsible young man. However, the reality is that Michael greatly resents the discipline and is afraid of his father. He has little desire to obey his wishes and spends most of the weekend avoiding his dad.

Even a casual observer can see the connection between Paul's seeming lack of love and Michael's lack of respect. The father's harsh words and angry tones might be tolerated by a child who felt secure in his father's love, but when the love tank is empty, as in Michael's case, such discipline creates anger and bitterness rather than responsibility.

If Michael felt secure in his father's love, he would know that the discipline he received was, at least in Paul's mind, for his well-being. But since he does not feel loved, he views his dad's discipline as an act of selfishness. More and more, Michael is seeing himself as little more than a bother to his dad, and this is seriously affecting his self-esteem.

Clearly it is crucial that you love your child unconditionally. You can do this much more effectively if you know and speak all the love languages. Every child needs this unconditional love to keep his or her emotional love tank full. Then you will be able to discipline with the best possible results. First things first, fellow parents. Practice unconditional love; then discipline.

HOW A CHILD LOVES

Before we are able to effectively discipline a child in love, we need to ask two questions:

1. How does a child love?
2. What does my child need when he misbehaves?

Well, how does a child love? In an immature fashion. In contrast, adults seek to love in an unconditional manner. Often we fail and settle for what is called a reciprocating love. For instance, Ryan has a deep affection for Robin, whom he wants to fall in love with him. Wanting to put his best foot forward, he tries to be pleasant, calm, helpful, kind, respectful, and considerate to her. Because he is not sure of Robin's love, he does not resort to immature behavior but seeks to earn her love. This rational approach to obtaining love is called reciprocating love because Ryan is doing his best to secure Robin's love in return.

But a child loves with neither reciprocating nor unconditional love. Being immature, a child loves in a self-oriented fashion. She is instinctively aware of her own need to feel loved—to have a full emotional love tank. She is not aware that her parents also have love tanks that need to be filled. Her only real concern is the status of her own love tank. When it is on low or empty, she is compelled to frantically ask, "Do you love me?" How her parents answer that question determines a great deal about the child's behavior, since the main cause of misbehavior is an empty emotional tank.

Some parents think a child should try to earn their love and affection with good behavior, but this just isn't possible. A child by nature continually tests our love by his or her behavior. He is asking, "Do you love me?" If we respond, "Yes, I love you," and fill his love tank, we take the pressure off and make it unnecessary for him to continue testing our love. We also make it much easier to control his behavior. However, if we fall into the trap of thinking our child should "earn" our love by good behavior, we will be continually frustrated. We will also see our child as bad, as disrespectful and unloving, when actually he needs to be reassured of our love.

WHEN A CHILD MISBEHAVES

When a child asks through his behavior, "Do you love me?" we may not like the behavior. If the child feels desperate enough, his behavior will turn inappropriate. Nothing makes a child more desperate than a lack of love. However, it does not make sense to demand good behavior from a child without first making sure he feels loved.

The second question we must ask in order to discipline with love is, "What does my child need when she misbehaves?" Instead, when a child misbehaves, many parents ask, "What can I do to correct her behavior?" If they ask that question, the logical answer is, "Punishment." This is one reason that punishment is so overused, rather than parents' selecting more appropriate ways of training a child. When we resort to punishment first, later we cannot easily consider the real needs of the child. A child will not feel loved if we handle misbehavior this way.

However, when we ask, "What does this child need?" we can proceed rationally and decide on a proper course. A child who misbehaves has a need. To overlook the need behind the misbehavior can prevent us from doing the right thing. Asking ourselves, "What can I do to correct my child's behavior?" often leads to thoughtless punishment. Asking, "What does my child need?" lets us proceed with confidence that we will handle the situation well.

WHY A CHILD MISBEHAVES: AN EMPTY LOVE TANK

When your child misbehaves and you have asked yourself, "What does my child need?" the next question should be, "Does this child need her love tank filled?" It is so much easier to discipline a child if she feels genuinely loved, particularly if the cause of the misbehavior is an empty love tank. At such a time, you need to keep the love languages in mind, especially physical touch and quality time, and the use of eye contact.

When a child obviously misbehaves, what he has done should not be condoned. However, if we deal with it wrongly—either too harshly or too permissively—we will have further problems with that child, and those problems will worsen as he grows older. Yes, we need to discipline (train) a child toward good behavior, but the first step in that process is not punishment.

Young children are not subtle about asking for our love. They are noisy and often do things that seem inappropriate to an adult way of thinking. When we realize that they are really pleading for us to spend time with them, to hold them, to give ourselves to them in a personal manner, we will remember that they are children and that we have the precious responsibility to fill their love tanks first, and then train them to move on in their journey.

WHY A CHILD MISBEHAVES: PHYSICAL PROBLEMS

But what do we do when misbehavior is not caused by an empty love tank?

After you have asked yourself, "What does this child need?" and you have determined that the child's love tank is not depleted, ask yourself, "Is this a physical problem?" The second most common cause of misbehavior is a physical problem, and the younger the child, the more behavior is affected by physical needs. "Is my child in pain? Hungry or thirsty? Fatigued? Ill?" Misbehavior cannot be condoned, even if it is caused by a physical problem, but the problem behavior can usually be quickly relieved if its source is physical.

A CHILD'S REMORSE, A PARENT'S FORGIVENESS

Let's assume that you determine that your child's misbehavior is not caused by physical reasons. What's the next question? "Does my child feel sorry for what he has done?" When a child feels genuinely sorry for what he has done, there is no need to proceed further. He has learned and repented; punishment now could be destructive. If your child is truly sorry and shows genuine remorse, you should rejoice. This means his conscience is alive and well.

What controls a child's (or adult's) behavior when he doesn't have to behave appropriately? Right: a healthy conscience. And what is the raw material from which a normal conscience is formed? Guilt. A certain amount of guilt is necessary for the development of a healthy conscience. And what will wipe away guilt, as clean as a new slate? You guessed it—punishment, especially corporal punishment. However, punish the child when he already feels genuinely guilty for his behavior, and you hinder his ability to develop a good conscience. In such a situation, punishment usually produces only anger and resentment.

When your child is truly sorry for her misbehavior, instead of punishing her, forgive her. In your example of forgiving her, you are teaching beautiful lessons about forgiveness she can take into her adult years. By experiencing forgiveness from her parents, she is learning to forgive herself and later to forgive someone else. What a beautiful gift this is. Have you seen a child who was truly remorseful about a wrong she did and then experienced a parent's forgiveness? This is a rare and unforgettable experience. The love that flows from the child's heart is overwhelming.

The only other way you can teach your child how to forgive is to ask forgiveness when you have wronged her. While you should do this occasionally, it should not be necessary often. If it is, you are unduly offending your child and not learning from your own mistakes.

FIVE IDEAS ON CONTROLLING YOUR CHILD'S BEHAVIOR

As parents we are responsible for so much that happens with our children, often more than we want to admit. We can learn ways to help our children avoid bad behavior and subsequent punishment. Here are five methods you can use to effectively control your child's behavior. Two of these are positive, two are negative, and one is neutral. As you read this section, you will want to think about the methods of control that you have employed with your children; you may want to change or add to your approach.

1. Making Requests

Making requests is a very important, positive means of controlling behavior. It greatly benefits both parent and child. Requests are pleasant to the child and help to ease the anger that may be stirred by a parent's commands. And it is so much easier for parents to be pleasant when using requests, thereby remaining "kind but firm."

When you make requests, you are sending three nonverbal messages to your child. The first is that you respect his feelings. You are saying, "I respect the fact that you have feelings, and your feelings about this matter in particular." The second nonverbal message is the fact that you realize your child has a brain and is able to form opinions. "I respect that you have an opinion about this."

The third message is the best of all. Requests tell your child that you expect her to take responsibility for her own behavior. This kind of responsibility is so lacking today. Your child can learn to be a responsible person when you give her the opportunity to do so. By the use of requests, you are guiding and encouraging her to take responsibility.

A child who is raised in this way comes to feel that he is in partnership with his parents in the molding of his character. This kind of child rearing is not permissiveness. The parent is not giving up authority or respect. In fact, the child will have much greater respect for his parents because he will feel that they are not simply telling him what to do but are interested primarily in what is best for him.

Also, requests are the best way of giving instructions. Since requests are more pleasant, thoughtful, and considerate than commands, you can use them to instruct your child almost endlessly. No other method of control allows this.

2. Issuing Commands

Issuing commands is necessary and appropriate at times. Requests are vastly superior when you have a choice, but commands are necessary when requests fail. Then you must be more forceful. Commands are a negative means of control because they require harsher tones than requests, with a downward voice inflection at the end of the statement. This combination almost always elicits irritation, anger, and resentment in the child, especially if used frequently. Also, the nonverbal messages that accompany commands are generally negative. Because you are telling a child what to do, with no choices or opportunity for feedback or discussion, you are conveying that the child's feelings and opinions are not important to you. Most of all, you are taking all the responsibility on yourself and essentially saying, "It doesn't matter what your feelings or opinions are about this. I don't expect you to take responsibility for your own behavior. I simply expect you to do what I am telling you."

The more you use authoritarian techniques such as commands, scolding, nagging, or screaming, the less effective you become. But if you normally use pleasant requests, then the occasional use of commands will generally be effective.

As parents, you have only so much authority. If you waste it being negative, you will not have enough left for the difficult, critical times. *Being kind but firm* not only conserves your authority, but it *enhances your authority, because you are gaining your children's respect and love as well as their gratitude.*

Children are great observers. They see and hear how other parents resort to unpleasant, authoritarian, and angry discipline with their children. When you are kind but firm with them, you can't imagine how much they appreciate you and how thankful they are to have you as their parents!

3. Gentle Physical Manipulation

Gentle physical manipulation can move a child in the appropriate direction. It's especially effective with young children who often do things that are not necessarily wrong—but are not to your preference. For instance, the negativism of two-year-olds can be easily confused with defiance. "No," Henry says, but then he will do what you request of him. Sometimes there is a delay after Henry says it, and then he responds to your request. It may seem to you that he is being defiant, but this is not so. Negativism in two-year-olds is a normal step of development, one way the child begins to separate psychologically from his mother or father.

This simple ability to say no is important. If you punish a small child for this, you are not only hurting him but directly interfering with his normal development. Please be careful not to confuse negativism with defiance. They are completely separate.

Let's say that you want your three-year-old daughter to come to you. You begin with a request, "Come to me, will you, Honey?" Your child answers, "No." You move to a command, "Come to me now!" Again she answers, "No." At this point it is a real temptation to punish her, but you should resist. Instead of taking a great risk and hurting your child, why not gently guide her to where you want her to be? If she resists, then you know it may be defiance and you can take an appropriate course. But, the vast majority of the time, you will discover that the child was not being defiant but was just saying no. And you haven't hurt a thing.

Negativism usually starts when children are two, but you can see examples of it in virtually every age. When you are not sure how to handle a situation, you can try gentle physical manipulation. It is particularly helpful when a small child acts up in a public place. Instead of giving in to frustration, her parents can simply move her on.

4. Punishment

Punishment is the most negative and also the most difficult method of control. First, the punishment must fit the crime because children are so aware of fairness. They know when a punishment is too lenient or severe. They can also detect inconsistency in their parents' attitudes toward the children in the family.

Second, the punishment may not be appropriate for the particular child. Sending a child to his room, for example, may feel very painful to one sibling and seem like a playtime to another. Third, punishment brings with it variation, since parents often rely on their feelings when they are dishing out a punishment. When everything is going their way and they are feeling good, they tend to be more lenient. On bad days, when a parent isn't feeling very good, the punishment meted out is harsher.

As difficult as it may be for you to decide when and how punishment should be used, you still must be prepared to use it and to use it appropriately. This can be facilitated by planning ahead so that you can avoid the "punishment trap." This means sitting down with a spouse or good friend to decide appropriate punishments for various offenses. Such planning will keep your anger in check when your child does something that upsets you.

When your child misbehaves and you quickly ask yourself the

questions we suggested earlier, and come up with negatives on all of them (including a two-year-old's constant "No"), you should ask one more question, "Is this child being defiant?" Defiance is openly resisting and challenging parental authority.

Of course, defiance cannot be permitted and the behavior must be corrected. But a child's defiance does not automatically mean that punishment is indicated. You want to avoid the punishment trap. If a request will break the defiance, and it often does, great. If gentle physical manipulation or a command is appropriate, good. If punishment is indicated, do it with care.

Finally, do not use punishment as your primary way of disciplining your young child or teenager. You will provoke great amounts of needless anger. You will also force your child to "stuff" his anger; he may develop passive-aggressive attitudes and behaviors, trying to get back at you indirectly. (We will discuss passive-aggressive behavior in chapter 10.)

5. Behavior Modification

Behavior modification can also control a child's behavior. It utilizes positive reinforcement (placing a positive element into a child's environment), negative reinforcement (withdrawing a positive element from the child's environment), and punishment (placing a negative element into the child's environment). An example of positive reinforcement is to reward a child for an appropriate behavior by giving her a piece of candy or fruit. One negative reinforcement could be withdrawing television privileges from a child for inappropriate behavior. An example of punishment (sometimes called aversive technique) would be sending a child to his room.

Behavior modification can be helpful at times, particularly for specific, recurring behavioral problems for which a child shows no remorse. But we believe it should be used sparingly. If parents over-use behavior modification, their child will not feel loved. The first reason for this is that the very foundation of behavior modification is conditional—the child receives a reward only if he behaves a certain way. Second, behavior modification does not deal with a child's feelings or emotional needs and cannot convey unconditional love. If parents control their child's behavior primarily by trying to modify it, the child will develop a warped value system in which he does things primarily for reward. A "what's in it for me?" orientation will follow.

Behavior modification can also teach children to use the same method on their parents. They will do what the parents wish in order to get what they want. This leads to manipulation.

Because of all the cautions about this method, you may be surprised that we suggest using it at all. Again, it can help with specific, recurring behavioral problems for a defiant child. However, working with a system of rewards takes time, consistency, effort, and persistence.

LOVE: BEFORE AND AFTER PUNISHMENT

Because discipline is most effective when it happens in the context of love, it is wise to give a child a conscious expression of love both before and after administering punishment. We have noted that the most effective way to communicate love is by using the child's primary love language, so speak it even when you must correct or punish the child.

Larry is an electrical engineer and by nature his personality is quite rigid. In his early years of parenting, he tended to be stern and matter-of-fact in disciplining his children. After learning about the five love languages, he determined that his son's primary love language was physical touch. He tells how he applied this in disciplining his son. "Kevin had broken the neighbor's window while playing baseball in the backyard. He knew it was against the rules to play baseball there—the park was just a block away and the place to play ball. On several occasions, we had talked about the dangers of playing ball in the backyard. When our neighbor saw Kevin hit the ball that broke the window, he called my wife to inform us.

"After I got home, I calmly went into Kevin's room where he was working on his computer. I walked over and started rubbing his shoulders. In a minute or so, he turned from the computer and gave me his attention. 'Stand up,' I said. 'I want to hug you.' I wrapped my arms around him as I said, 'I've got to do something really tough, and I want you to know that I love you more than anything.'

"I kept hugging him for a long minute—it felt good to be close. Then I released him and said, 'Mom called today to tell me what happened to Mr. Scott's window. I know it was an accident, but you are well aware of the rule about not playing baseball in the yard. Therefore, I have to discipline you for breaking that rule. It hurts me to do this, but it is for your good. No baseball for the next two weeks. And you must use your money to pay for repairing the Scotts' window. We'll call the window company to find out how much it will cost.'

"Then I hugged him again. I know he felt my tears running down his neck. I said, 'I love you, Buddy.' And he said, 'I love you too, Dad.' I left the room, knowing I had done the right thing; somehow it felt so much better when I assured him of my love before and after the discipline. Knowing that physical touch was his primary love language, I felt the discipline was received in a positive manner. I remember well previous times when I have disciplined him out of my anger and said harsh and bitter words and sometimes spanked him in a heat of rage. I thank God that I now know a better way."

If Kevin's love language had been words of affirmation, Larry's encounter with him might have gone something like this: "Kevin, I need to talk with you for a few minutes. I want you to know how much I love you and appreciate the hard work you do at school. I know when you come home you want to relax, and that you enjoy playing baseball. You usually follow our house rules and I really appreciate that. It is rare that I have to discipline you. What I am trying to say is that what we need to talk about is an isolated incident and not typical of your behavior, and I'm grateful for that.

"You probably know that Mr. Scott called your mother this afternoon and told her that he saw you hit the baseball that broke his window. While it was an accident, you do know the rule about playing baseball in the backyard. It is hard for me to do this, but because you disobeyed, I have to discipline you. No baseball for two weeks. And, you will have to use your own money to pay for having the Scotts' window repaired. I'll call the window company to find out what it will cost.

"Do you understand that I am not angry with you? I know that you didn't mean to break the window, and also that you probably weren't thinking when you started playing ball in the yard. I love you very much and I'm proud of you. I know you will learn a good lesson from this experience." Their conversation may end with a hug, but the primary expression of love is in the words of affirmation both before and after the discipline.

Using your child's primary love language doesn't mean that you may not also use some of the other love languages; it does mean that you are giving your child the most effective expression of love you possibly can, both before and after the discipline. Because you know that you will be showing love to your child, you will probably be more careful about the type of discipline you choose to administer, and the way in which you do it.

RESPECTING YOUR CHILD'S LOVE LANGUAGE

Understanding your child's primary love language will help you choose the best method of discipline. In most cases, do not use a form of discipline that is directly related to your child's primary love language. Respect the child's love language by not selecting it as a method of discipline. Such discipline will not have the desired effect and may actually cause extreme emotional pain. The message your child will receive is not one of loving correction but one of painful rejection.

For example, if your child's love language is words of affirmation and you use condemning words as a form of discipline, your words will communicate not only that you are displeased with a certain behavior but also that you do not love your child. Critical words can be painful to any child, but to this child, they will be emotionally devastating. Thus Ben, age sixteen, told us his father didn't love him, citing his dad's discipline, which included a raised voice and cutting words:

> **If your daughter's primary love language is quality time, you don't want to discipline her with isolation.**

"If I happen to do something he thinks is wrong, his screaming can go on for hours. I remember the day he told me he wasn't sure I was his son because he couldn't believe his son would do anything that terrible. I don't really know if I am his son, but I know that he doesn't love me."

As he talked further, it became obvious that Ben's primary love language was words of affirmation. When his father used words to communicate his displeasure with Ben's behavior, he destroyed the boy's sense of being loved.

Be careful. If your daughter's primary love language is quality time, you don't want to discipline her with isolation, such as sending her to her room each time she misbehaves. If it's physical touch, don't discipline by withholding your hugs. We remember Carlos, a ten-year-old whose primary love language is physical touch. He often walks up behind his mother and puts his arms around her or rubs her shoulders. His mother is also physically demonstrative and often communicates love to Carlos by physical touch. But Carlos's father, Joe, was raised in a home where spanking was the normal method of discipline; consequently, that is his primary method of discipline when Carlos disobeys.

These spankings are not abusive, in that they do not break the skin or leave Carlos with welts. However, when Carlos receives one of Joe's spankings, he may cry for three hours. What his father does not understand is that he is taking his son's primary love language, physical touch, and using it in a negative way. Consequently, Carlos feels not only punished but also unloved. His dad never hugs him after a spanking, for this would seem incongruous in his philosophy of discipline.

Joe is sincere in his efforts to discipline his son, but he doesn't recognize how much emotional distance he is putting between himself and Carlos. As parents, we must constantly be reminded that the purpose of discipline is to correct the wrong behavior and to help a child develop self-discipline. If we do not apply the love language concept, we may well destroy a child's sense of being loved, in our efforts to correct bad behavior. Understanding the primary love language of your child can make your discipline far more effective.

9

Learning and the Love Languages

Parents are a child's first and most important teachers. Researchers now agree that the optimum time for the stimulation of basic learning abilities in a child is before the age of six. Dr. Burton White, a famed pioneer in early learning research and the founder of the Harvard Preschool Project, says, "It appears that a first-rate educational experience during the first three years of life is required if a person is to develop to his/her full potential."[1] And sociologists and educators, convinced such stimulation of the very young can spur learning abilities, have created programs such as Head Start designed to help disadvantaged children during their preschool years.

Yes, we parents are the primary teachers. And one of our primary teaching aids is proper discipline, administered with love.

In chapter 8, we considered discipline as guiding to maturity. Now let's consider the other half of the classical idea of discipline: teaching our children. True discipline can help to develop a child's intellect and social skills that will serve him for a lifetime.

The increased awareness in recent years of the importance of early childhood learning underscores our crucial role as parents in our child's developing intelligence. This does not mean you must conduct formal lessons with your young child. But you should try to understand your child's innate drive to learn, to explore, and then to satisfy his developing brain's urgent need for sensory stimuli and enjoyable learning experiences.

Many parents watch their child's primary occupation of play and think learning can be left for first grade. But small children love to learn. They are born with an innate hunger for learning that remains strong—unless adults bore, spank, train, or discourage it out of them. A careful observation of infants and toddlers reveals that most of their activity is not merely child's play. Rather, our little ones are working at learning a new skill, whether it is to flip from the stomach to the back; to crawl; to pull up and later walk; or to touch, feel, and taste the world around them.

Once they learn to talk, their minds are filled with questions, and three- and four-year-olds can ask dozens of questions every day. When they reach the imitative stage and pretend to be adults, they seldom copy grown-ups at play. Rather, they imitate adults at work: teaching, driving a truck, being a doctor or nurse, caring for babies, working as a "businessman," and more. If you observe your child's activities for just one day and ask, "What seems to make her happiest? What holds her attention the longest?" you will likely find that it is an activity in which she is learning.

THE KEY TO YOUR CHILD'S LEARNING: YOU

Children discover life through the five senses. A home environment that is rich in stimulation of vision, hearing, touch, taste, and smell will feed their natural desire to discover and learn. Language development depends to a great extent on the verbal stimulation children receive from adults in these early years. Thus, talking to them and encouraging them to say words cooperates with their natural desire to learn. Cheering their efforts to say words and giving corrective feedback are part of the process. In this kind of rich verbal environment, their vocabulary grows and their ability to use sentences develops. They later learn to employ this skill to express emotions, thoughts, and desires.

What is true of verbal development is true in all areas of intellectual growth. If the home does not provide this kind of basic intellectual stimulation, a child is likely to be handicapped in his later learning, and the prognosis for his educational development is poor. School programs offer only a small compensation for an unstimulating home environment.

A supportive environment and attitude will help our children learn at home. Children are more emotional than cognitive—that is, they remember feelings more readily than they do facts. This means that your children remember how they felt in a particular situation much more easily than they recall the details of the event. For instance, a child listening to a story will remember exactly how she felt long after she forgets the lesson.

Your daughter may forget the details but remember the teacher. In your teaching, this means treating her with respect, kindness, and concern. It means making her feel good about herself, and ensuring that you never criticize or humiliate her. When a teaching situation is boring or degrading, a child is likely to reject even the best teaching, especially if morality or ethics are involved. When you respect your child, she will respect you and your viewpoint.

The key to your child's learning is you, from infancy on through all the years of formal training. Learning is a complex feat that is influenced by many factors. One of the strongest of these is your total involvement.

HOW THE LOVE LANGUAGES AID LEARNING

The most important fact to know about a child's learning ability is this: For a child to be able to learn well at any age, he must be at the emotional maturational level of that particular age. As the child grows, his ability to learn increases because of several factors, the most important of which is his emotional maturity. And parents have the greatest effect on the child's emotional growth.

This is not to say that all learning problems are the fault of parents, since many factors can affect a child's learning ability. However, emotional development can make a tremendous difference in the child's learning readiness and process, and this is where parents can help the most. We can prime our child's learning pump by continually filling his emotional tank.

Many parents do not realize that a child can fall behind emotionally.

As you consistently speak the five languages of love—physical touch, words of affirmation, quality time, receiving gifts, and acts of service—you are giving your child much intellectual stimulation. In the early years, when you probably don't know your child's primary love language, you regularly give all five. In so doing, you are not only meeting your child's emotional need for love but are also providing him with the physical and intellectual stimuli needed to develop his emerging interests. Although your emphasis is on love, you are also teaching and training your child.

Parents who do not take time to speak the five love languages, but simply seek to meet a child's physical needs, are neglecting her intellectual and social development. A child who is starved for love and acceptance from his parents will have little motivation to accept the challenges of learning in the early years or later in school.

Many parents do not realize that a child can fall behind emotionally. And it is certainly possible for a child to fall behind to such an extent that he can never catch up. What a tragedy! A child's emotional maturation affects everything else—his self-esteem, emotional security, ability to cope with stress and change, ability to socialize, and the ability to learn.

Perhaps nowhere else is the connection between love and learning more clearly demonstrated than when a child's parents separate or divorce. This traumatic break ruptures the child's emotional tank and drains his interest in learning. In place of love, the child often feels confusion and fear, neither of which are good companions for learning. A child whose parents have divorced will usually show lessened academic interest for several months until some measure of security and assurance of love can be restored to his world. Sadly enough, some children never fully recover.

As parents, we have the greatest influence in a child's life. If you are a single parent, by practicing your child's love language, you can help to restore your child's sense of security. (A cooperative ex-spouse also will help.) This full love tank will then enable him to reach each succeeding emotional level in time to be ready to take the next step in learning.

"TIGER MOTHERS" AND OTHERS

Studies consistently show that parental involvement in education helps children thrive in school. Recently, books like *The Battle*

Hymn of the Tiger Mother, by Amy Chua, have shone a spotlight on the extremes some parents go to in order to ensure their children's academic success, and have sparked debate about exactly how involved parents should be. In an era where there is intense attention to American competitiveness in a global marketplace and concern about American student achievement as compared to students in other countries, parents feel unease about their roles and sometimes will go to extraordinary lengths to help their children succeed. At the same time, young people growing up in less-privileged environments fall further and further behind.

Often, the missing piece in these environments is the presence of a father. Research consistently demonstrates that greater attention from fathers results in less delinquent behavior and higher levels of education for the children. And while the children get blamed for delinquent behavior, it is usually the fathers who are the delinquent ones in relation to the children.

But whether you are married, remarried, or a single parent, as a parent concerned with giving your children the love they need, you want to be sure to spend the time necessary to fill their love tanks with all five love languages. You are the key to your children's ability to learn and succeed in every way. And you have a great advantage over people outside your family—you know and understand your own children and have the home environment in which you can meet their needs.

IF YOUR CHILD IS ANXIOUS

A child who is doing well emotionally will have the concentration, motivation, and energy she needs to use her abilities to the maximum. In contrast, if she is distressed with anxiety or melancholy, or feels unloved, she probably will have problems with concentration and attention span and feel a decrease in energy. It will be more difficult for her to keep her mind on the task at hand. Studying may seem uninteresting. She will tend to be preoccupied with herself and her emotional needs, and her ability to learn will suffer.

If this anxiety continues, it will become more evident when the child enters a new learning experience. Such learning-related anxiety often appears among children who are moving from the third to the fourth grade. This grade step usually involves a change in the content and in the methods of teaching. The primary difference is the move from thinking and learning concretely to the inclusion of thinking and learning abstractly. Concrete learning deals with plain facts: Baltimore is in the state of Maryland. Abstract thinking is symbolic: words and phrases represent ideas and concepts. Moving from concrete to abstract thinking is a huge step, and not all children can accomplish it on cue.

When a child fails to make this step with ease, he suffers in many ways. He cannot fully understand the content of the lessons. He senses that he is falling behind, and this damages his self-esteem as he feels inferior to his peers. Unless this is corrected quickly, the child will develop depression, more anxiety, and will begin to feel like an overall failure. Because the move to fourth grade is one of the most critical periods of academic transition, it is worth special notice by parents.

Your child's level of emotional maturity can make a significant difference in how he or she weathers this transition. By "emotional maturity" we mean the ability to control their anxiety, withstand stress, and maintain balance during times of change. The more your children can do these things, the better they can learn. And the best way to help your children mature emotionally and maintain a good motivational level for their age is to keep their emotional love tanks full.

One sign of anxiety in children is an inability to easily make eye contact. An extremely anxious child will have problems approaching others, adults as well as peers. The emotionally deprived child will have difficulty in the simplest communication. Routine learning is bound to be affected by this tension and anxiety.

Some of these children have been helped by special attention from their teachers that includes eye contact and physical contact. As their emotional needs are met, their fears and anxieties will lessen and their security and confidence increase. They are then able to learn. Of course, it is far preferable for these needs to be met at home by loving parents.

HOW CAN YOU MOTIVATE YOUR CHILD?

A question parents often ask is, "How can I motivate my child?" We can motivate only after we have filled our children's love tanks and trained them to manage their anger. Failing these two essentials, it is nearly impossible to understand how to motivate children.

The key to motivating a child is to get her to take responsibility for her own behavior. A child who will not or cannot take this responsibility cannot be motivated. A child who is taking responsibility for herself is motivated.

Encourage Your Child's Interests

You can help your child to be responsible (and therefore motivated) in two ways. The first is to patiently observe what your child is drawn to; that is, what your child enjoys, appreciates, or likes to do. Then you can encourage him in that direction. If you see an interest in your child in studying music, you can encourage that. But the key is to let the child take the initiative. When parents take the initiative to convince a child to take music lessons, the results are rarely positive.

Allow Your Child to Take Responsibility

A second way to help your child be motivated is to remember both you and your child cannot take responsibility for the same thing at the same time. If you wait and allow your child to take the initiative, she may then be motivated because you have allowed her to take responsibility. If you take the initiative and try to convince her to do something, *you* are assuming responsibility. A child is seldom motivated when this happens.

Let's apply this to the area of homework and grades. Most children go through periods when doing homework becomes a problem. This is especially true when passive-aggressive behavior enters the picture. And remember, a certain amount of passive-aggressive behavior is normal in thirteen- to fifteen-year-olds.

Passive-aggressive behavior goes for the jugular; that is, it aims at what will most upset the parents. Most parents care about their kids getting good grades. So that the more importance parents place on schoolwork, the more the child will tend to resist it. And remember this: *The more responsibility the parent takes regarding the homework, the less the child will take.* And, the less responsibility the child takes in doing his homework, the less motivated he will be.

If you want your child to take responsibility and be highly motivated, you must realize that homework is your child's responsibility, not yours. How do you accomplish this? Let your child know that you will be happy to help with his homework if he asks you. Since you want him to take responsibility for his work, even when he asks for help, you want to avoid taking any of the work on yourself, but want to place it back on your child.

For example, let's say your son has a math problem. You shouldn't solve the problem for him. Instead, you can look in the math book and show him the explanations for doing that type of problem. Then you can hand back the book so that he is able to assume responsibility for doing the problem. Eventually this will teach him to take more responsibility for himself. If you feel that the teacher has not adequately explained the concepts, you might suggest that your child ask for help the next day.

Of course, there will be times when you must clarify points of confusion or give a child additional information. This is fine as long as you are not assuming the responsibility your child should be taking. If you realize that you have been intensely involved in your child's homework, try to gradually shift responsibility to your child. You may see a temporary reduction in grades, but your child's ability to assume the responsibility and become self-sufficient will be well worth it. As you take this approach, your child should need less help as time goes on. And you can spend some of your time together exploring subjects of special interest to you both that are not included in a school curriculum.

Helping a child to be well motivated by permitting her to take both initiative and responsibility for her own behavior seems to be a well-concealed secret today. Most children are placed in a position where a parent or teacher takes the initiative and then assumes responsibility for her learning. Adults do this because they genuinely care for the children and mistakenly believe that the more they take initiative and responsibility, the more they are doing for the children. However, this is a serious mistake.

Using Your Child's Love Language

Your children will reach their highest motivation and success in learning at school when they are secure in your love. If you understand your children's primary love language, you can enhance their daily experiences by speaking their primary language as they leave for school in the morning and as they return in the afternoon. Those are two important times in the lives of school-age children. To be touched emotionally by their parents on leaving and returning home gives them security and courage to face the challenges of the day.

Julia is nine years old. After her mother, Kelly, learned about the five love languages, she made some changes in their daily routine. "I simply can't believe the difference it made in Julia's life," she told us later. "Even after I heard about the love language concept and discovered that Julia's language was acts of service, I never thought that applying this concept would be that helpful at school. But then, a friend mentioned that she was speaking her child's love language before her daughter left for school and when she came home in the afternoon. I decided to try this and the results were almost immediate.

"Mornings at our house were always rather hectic; my husband left home at 7:00, Julia's bus came at 7:30, and I left about 7:50. We all did our own thing and about the only meaningful contact we had with each other was a goodbye as we left the house."

Knowing that Julia valued acts of service, Kelly asked Julia, "If I could do one thing for you in the morning that would help you, what would it be?"

Julia thought a moment. "Um . . . I guess having all my stuff ready to go. Because it seems I'm always looking for things, then I have to run for the bus."

The next morning Kelly made sure Julia's lunch, homework, and anything else she needed were safely stowed in her backpack, which waited by the door. Soon, she said, "I could tell a difference in her morning attitude. She even said thank you most days. And, when she left for school, she seemed to be in a better mood.

"Three days later, I did an act of service in the afternoons when she returned home. The first day I had bought some fruit at the farmers' market. When she came in and dropped her backpack, I said, 'Julia, I got those apples you like. Want to try one?' Then we sat down to talk about her day. The next afternoon, I had found a book of hers she had thought was lost. When she came in, I said, 'Look on the kitchen table.' I had left her book there and she said, 'Oh, thank you! Where did you find it?'"

Kelly began listening to her daughter's requests more attentively, writing them down. And the after-school time became a highlight of their day.

"All of this began four months ago," she said. "The biggest difference I notice is that when we talk about school, her comments are much more positive than they were before. It seems to me that she is having a better time and is more motivated than she was. Also, I feel that our relationship is closer."

If Julia's primary love language had been physical touch, then a warm hug as she left for the bus each morning and open arms as she walked into the house in the afternoon would have served the same emotional purpose. Of course, she would have enjoyed the treats too.

Perhaps you cannot be home when your children return after school. If so, the next best thing is to show a sincere expression of love when you walk in the door. If your last encounter in the morning and your first encounter in the evening is to speak the primary love language of your children, you will be performing one of your most meaningful deeds of the day. And, this just may have a positive impact on their motivation for learning.

10

Anger and Love

A nger and love. The two are more closely related than most of us
want to admit. We get angry at the people we love. You may be
surprised to find a chapter on anger in a book about love. But the truth
is, often we feel anger and love at the same time.

Anger is the most troublesome emotion in family life. It can lead
to marital conflict and to the verbal and physical abuse of children.
Mishandled anger is at the root of most of society's problems. Yet we
must realize that anger has a positive place in our lives and in rearing our children. Not all anger is evil. You can feel anger because you
want justice and care for someone's (including your child's) welfare.
The ultimate and righteous purpose of anger is to motivate us to set
things right and to correct evil. Thus, angry mothers formed MADD,
Mothers Against Drunk Driving, to try to stop this scourge on our
highways. Their organization began after one woman channeled her
anger over her child's death by an intoxicated driver in a positive

manner, lobbying for tougher laws against drunken motorists.

However, anger more commonly creates problems than solves them. As an emotion, anger is not always expressed for righteous reasons. It often becomes irrational and we do not control it; it controls us. In the heat of anger, people often throw reason to the wind and take a destructive course that actually makes things worse. Also, we don't always judge properly what is the greatest right for ourselves and other people, or we seek to correct wrongs in selfish ways.

The primary lifetime threat to your child is their own anger.

Anger is a little-understood emotion—why we feel it, how we express it, and how we can change the way we deal with our frustrations. Unless we as parents know what anger is and how we can handle it in appropriate ways, we will not be able to teach our children what to do when they feel angry. Yes, *when*, because all of us, parents and children, get angry every day.

It may surprise you that the primary lifetime threat to your child is their own anger. If your child does not handle his own anger well, it will damage or destroy him. The mishandling of anger is related to every present and future problem your child may have—from poor grades to damaged relationships to possible suicide. It is imperative that you do all you can to safeguard your child now and in the future.

However, the good news is that if your child learns to handle anger well, he will have a great advantage in life. Most of life's problems will be averted and your child will be more able to use anger to his advantage, rather than to have it work against him.

IS THIS YOUR FAMILY?

Equally important, we parents must learn to handle our own anger as we respond to our children. Few adults have mastered appropriate ways to handle anger. One reason is that most anger is expressed subconsciously, below the level of our awareness. Another is that few adults have made the transition from immature to mature means of dealing with anger. Typically this affects our dealings with our spouse and children. Consider how the Jacksons deal with their anger.

After a day's work, a tired Jeff Jackson is checking Facebook on his iPhone in the den. A tired Ellen Jackson is cleaning up after dinner. Neither is very happy with the other. Will comes in and asks Mom for some cookies. She is not in a cookie-giving mood and says, "You didn't finish your supper and so you can't have anything else." Feeling the cause is lost, Will goes to the den where he finds a candy jar. Dad asks, "What are you doing? You heard your mother. No candy!"

Will leaves the room but returns in five minutes, bouncing his basketball. "Can I go to Jack's house?"

"No, you can't. You haven't finished your homework. And stop bouncing that ball!"

Will takes his ball and leaves. In five minutes he is back, this time bouncing his ball in the kitchen. "Mom, I need a book to finish my homework and I didn't bring mine home. Jack has one. Can I go over there and borrow his?" Just then the basketball hits the table, knocking a glass to the floor.

Hearing this, Jeff is out of his chair and into the kitchen. "I told you to stop bouncing that ball!" He grabs Will by the hand and pulls him into the den where he starts flailing him on the bottom, yelling, "How many times do I have to tell you? You're going to learn to listen to me!"

Ellen is in the kitchen crying. She calls, "Stop it. Stop it. You're gonna kill him!" When Jeff stops, Will runs to his room, also crying. Dad plops onto the couch and stares at the TV. Mom goes to the bedroom, still crying. The family anger has not served a constructive purpose.

Many emotions were swirling in this household and everyone was angry. Ellen was angry at Jeff for not helping her clean up. Jeff was angry with Will for disobeying their house rule about the basketball. And Will was the angriest of all, because his dad's discipline was far out of line with his crime. Ellen was also angry at her husband's actions toward their son.

Nothing is resolved. Everything is worse. What Will does with his anger remains to be seen. Even if he shows compliance on the surface and acts as if everything is all right, you can be sure that his anger will show up later in his behavior.

"I HAVE A PROBLEM"

Now let's imagine this scene with a different response to anger.

Early in the evening, Ellen leaves the kitchen and joins Jeff in the den, speaking his primary love language for a moment, and then saying to him, "I have a problem. I'm feeling quite angry right now, but don't worry, I'm not going to attack you. I just need your help in solving my problem. Is this a good time to talk?" Then she may return to the kitchen or go to another room and read for a while.

When they do talk, Ellen calmly shares her sense of unfairness that he is not helping her clean up, especially since she worked all day too and then prepared supper. She tells him that she expects more of him and asks that he make a practice of helping her in the future.

If Ellen and Jeff had had this talk, Will's request for a cookie might have received a different response. When he bounced the ball for the second time in the kitchen, Dad could have come in and taken the ball in his hand, spoken Will's primary love language for a moment, explained to him his disobedience and let him know that his ball would be locked in the trunk of Dad's car for the next two days. Then he could have spoken his son's primary love language again for a moment. What a different situation there would have been in this home.

Parents who have not learned to control their own anger are not likely to train their children how to do it. And yet, this kind of training is essential for the well-being of children and of society. If you have never learned how to manage your own anger, we strongly urge you to get some help in this area, so that you will be able to teach your children by example and by word how to best handle their anger.

> **If you have never learned how to manage your own anger, we strongly urge you to get help in this area.**

THE RIGHT KIND OF ANGER

How your child learns to handle anger will largely influence the development of his personal integrity, one of the most important aspects of character. Train your child to manage anger appropriately and he will then be able to develop good character and strong integrity. However, if the child is not taught to handle anger in a mature way, he will always have pockets of immaturity in his character—that is, in his personal value systems, ethics, and morals. Such immaturity will manifest itself in a lack of integrity.

This lack will critically affect the child's spiritual development; the less able a child is to deal with anger well, the more antagonistic will be his attitude toward authority, including the authority of God. A child's immature handling of anger is a primary reason the child will reject the parent's spiritual values.

However, the good news is that when we parents do our job of training our children to manage their anger, we will see them thrive in life. Realize that anger itself is a normal human reaction; it is neither good nor bad. The problem is not the anger but the way it is managed. It can have beneficial results, if it energizes and motivates us to take action when we would otherwise remain silent.

We remember Jill, a shy fourteen-year-old who dreaded confrontations and conflict. She is truly a people-pleaser, and was struggling in her history class, where the teacher made a habit of putting down all religious faiths, especially Christianity. He frequently ridiculed well-known Christians whom Jill admired. As a Christian, Jill at first felt confused by her teacher's antagonism and later even began to question her own faith.

Then, about midyear, the teacher made a caustic remark about "preachers' kids." One of Jill's friends was the daughter of a pastor and this made Jill angry. In fact, she was furious! That evening she called some other Christian kids in the class and laid out a plan in which they agreed to participate. The next time the teacher began his belittling remarks, these students spoke up, though in a respectful way. They let the teacher know his comments were offensive. His first response was to try to ridicule the young people, but he soon realized how foolish he sounded and changed the subject. For the rest of the year, he made no more derogatory comments about religious faiths. Jill had used her anger constructively, to educate her teacher and to protect her personal freedom.

THE PASSIVE-AGGRESSIVE CHILD

Unfortunately, most people do not manage their anger as well as Jill did. A more common and destructive way to handle anger is called passive-aggressive behavior. Passive-aggressive behavior is an expression of anger that gets back at a person or group indirectly, or "passively." It is a subconscious determination to do exactly opposite of what an authority figure wants. An authority figure is a parent, teacher, minister, boss, policeman, laws, societal norms—any person or value system that represents authority. Of course, for a child or teenager, the primary authority figures are parents.

Ben, fifteen, is bright, has no learning problems, and is capable of getting good grades. He brings home his books most nights and does his homework. But he is angry at his parents, and he is bringing home grades well below his ability. His parents are frustrated. His behavior is a classic passive-aggressive response.

Why Ben Didn't Do His Homework

There are several ways for parents to decide if they are dealing with passive-aggressive behavior, and a correct identification is important, since there are many other reasons for behavioral problems. First, passive-aggressive behavior does not make sense. This was certainly true in Ben's case—with his ability and hard work, his poor grades were very difficult to understand.

Second, you can suspect passive-aggressive behavior when nothing you do to correct the behavior works. Because the purpose of passive-aggressive behavior is to upset the authority figure, no matter what action that authority figure takes, it will make no difference. Nothing that Ben's parents or teachers did improved his grades. They helped him with his homework, they promised to reward him for good grades, and they even tried punishment. Each new method seemed to improve the situation briefly, but in the long run, nothing worked. This is the reason passive-aggressive behavior is so difficult to deal with. Subconsciously, Ben was making sure that nothing would work, since the underlying purpose was to upset the authority figures.

Third, although the purpose of this behavior is to frustrate authority figures, the person acting in this way is the one who will ultimately be defeated and whose future and relationships will be seriously affected.

Passive-Aggressive Behavior during the Early Teen Years

There is only one period of life when passive-aggressive behavior is normal: early adolescence, when a child is thirteen to fifteen years old. And it can be considered normal only if it does not cause harm to anyone. It is essential that the child learns how to handle anger in a mature fashion and grows out of the passive-aggressive stage. If he does not, this behavior will become a permanent part of his character and personality for life, used against employers, spouse, children, and friends.

Today teenagers have many options for passive-aggressive behavior, and some of these are dangerous: drugs, violence, alcohol, crime, sexual activity resulting in venereal disease or pregnancy, school failure, and even suicide. Often, when the teens move out of this stage, serious life damage has been done.

Many parents have made the tragic mistake of thinking that all anger is wrong and should be disciplined out of children.

As parents, you need to distinguish between harmless passive-aggressive behavior and that which is abnormal and harmful. For example, toilet-papering trees is a normal outlet during a teen's passive-aggressive stage. A messy room may be aggravating, but it is harmless. Also, strenuous physical activities can help teenagers to satisfy their desire for excitement and danger. Teens may be helped through this stage by involvement in mountain climbing, rope courses, long-distance biking, and team or individual sports.

As you seek to help your young teenagers through this stage, remember that your objective is to train them to manage their anger by the time they are seventeen years old. They can't leave the passive-aggressive stage unless they learn other, more mature and acceptable ways to replace the behavior. Unfortunately, many people never grow out of this stage—passive-aggressive behavior among adults is all too common.

The truth is that most people do not understand anger or the ways in which it can be managed. Many parents have made the tragic mistake of thinking that all anger is wrong and should be disciplined out of children. This approach does not work and it does children no favors. It does not train children to handle their anger in constructive ways; consequently, they continue to mishandle it into adulthood, just as their parents did before them. Passive-aggressive behavior is a primary cause of failure in college, problems at work, and conflict in marriage.

Because passive-aggressive behavior is the hidden source of most of life's worst difficulties, we as parents must train our children and teens to manage anger appropriately. We can't discipline it out of them.

BEGIN EARLY

Obviously, you can't wait until the teenage years to teach your children about anger management. You have to begin when they are very young, although you can't expect them to be able to handle anger with any level of maturity until the age of six or seven.

Anger management is the most difficult part of parenting because children are limited in the ways they can express anger. They have only two options, verbal or behavioral expression, and both are difficult for parents to handle. Parents find it hard to understand that the anger must come out some way—that it cannot be totally bottled up.

As a result, many parents respond to children's expressions of anger in wrong and destructive ways.

As you consider the two options, recognize that it is better for your child to express anger verbally rather than behaviorally. When your child vents anger in words, you are able to train her in the direction of mature anger management. You want to avoid passive-aggressive behavior at all costs.

Until the age of six or seven, you are working primarily to keep passive-aggressive behavior from taking root in your child. The first and most important way you do this is to keep his emotional love tank full of unconditional love. The prime cause of anger and of misbehavior is an empty love tank. Speak your child's love language clearly and regularly and you will fill that tank and prevent passive-aggressive behavior from taking root. When that love tank is full, the child is under no pressure to display his unhappiness by asking, through his behavior, "Do you love me?" The child whose love tank is empty is compelled to ask, through misbehavior, "Do you love me?"

Next, realize that your children have no defense against parental anger. When you dump your anger on your child, it goes right down inside the child. If you do this often enough, this bottled anger will probably come out as passive-aggressive behavior. Listen to her calmly; let her express her anger verbally. It may not be pleasant to hear her anger, but it's preferable to her acting it out.

Unfortunately, when children let their anger out verbally, too many parents lash out and say something like, "How dare you talk to me like that? I never want to hear you speak to me that way again. Do you understand?" The children then have only two choices. They can obey and not express anger verbally, or they can disobey. What a corner to be in!

HELPING CHILDREN CLIMB THE ANGER LADDER

Thousands of parents have been helped in their understanding of a child's anger by visualizing an Anger Ladder. As you work with your children in the coming years, you will always be seeking to help them climb from one rung of the Anger Ladder to the next, away from the most negative expressions of anger to the more positive. The goal is to move the child from passive-aggressive behavior and verbal abuse to a calm, even pleasant response that seeks resolution. This is a long process that involves training, example, and patience.

You will notice that passive-aggressive behavior is at the bottom of the ladder. It represents totally unmanaged anger. Because this behavior is common during the teenage years, you will have to deal with that level at some point, but you should not let your teenage child stay there. If you do, you could be heading for serious problems.

You need to remind yourself that your child can climb only one rung at a time. If you want the process and training to be finished soon, this will be frustrating. You may wait some time before your child is ready to take the next step. This calls for patience and wisdom, but the results are well worth the wait. As you watch your child express anger, you need to identify where she is on the Anger Ladder, so that you will know the next step.

In the Campbell household, I remember one particularly unpleasant experience when my son, David, was thirteen. He verbalized his anger only when a particular event upset him. Sometimes he was verbalizing his anger at me in ways that I didn't want to hear. I had to do some self-talk. I knew letting him express that anger would help to determine where he was on the Anger Ladder. Inside myself I would say to him, *Attaboy, David, attaboy. Let that anger out, because when it is all out, I've got you.* Of course, I didn't say this to David.

Another reason I wanted the anger to come out was that as long as it was inside of David, it controlled the house. But once it was outside, he felt silly and I could regain control. He had gotten all the anger out verbally and was asking himself, "Now what do I do?" It was then that I was in a great position to train him.

Letting David roll those words out of his mouth helped in another way. The more anger he expressed verbally, the less there would be to come out in destructive attitudes and behaviors.

That will be true for your child too. Let him or her verbalize the anger and you'll see where the child stands on the Anger Ladder, and you can limit potential passive-aggressive behavior.

LET YOUR CHILD SHOW HER ANGER

Fellow parents, this way of dealing with children is not always easy to accept. Allowing a child to express anger verbally may seem permissive. It really is not. Remember that children of any age will naturally express anger in immature ways. You can't train them to express their anger in mature ways simply by getting upset at them and forcing them to stop venting their anger. If you do, their anger will be over-suppressed and passive-aggressive behavior will be the result.

If you want to train your children to manage anger in a mature fashion, you must *allow them to express it verbally, as unpleasant as that may be.* Remember, all anger must come out either verbally or behaviorally. If you don't allow it to come out verbally, passive-aggressive behavior will follow.

When your child speaks in anger, it does not necessarily mean that she is being disrespectful. To determine whether she is respectful, ask yourself, "What is the child's attitude toward my authority most of the time?" Most children are respectful over 90 percent of the time. If

THE ANGER LADDER

POSITIVE

1. PLEASANT • SEEKING RESOLUTION • FOCUSING ANGER ON SOURCE
   • HOLDING TO PRIMARY COMPLAINT • THINKING LOGICALLY

2. PLEASANT • FOCUSING ANGER ON SOURCE
   • HOLDING TO PRIMARY COMPLAINT • THINKING LOGICALLY

POSITIVE AND NEGATIVE

3. FOCUSING ANGER ON SOURCE • HOLDING TO PRIMARY COMPLAINT
   • THINKING LOGICALLY • Unpleasant, loud

4. HOLDING TO PRIMARY COMPLAINT • THINKING LOGICALLY
   • Unpleasant, loud • Displacing anger to other sources

5. FOCUSING ANGER ON SOURCE • HOLDING TO PRIMARY COMPLAINT
   • THINKING LOGICALLY • Unpleasant, loud • Verbal abuse

6. THINKING LOGICALLY • Unpleasant, loud
   • Displacing anger to other sources • Expressing unrelated complaints

PRIMARILY NEGATIVE

7. Unpleasant, loud • Displacing anger to other sources
   • Expressing unrelated complaints • Emotionally destructive behavior

8. Unpleasant, loud • Displacing anger to other sources
   • Expressing unrelated complaints • Verbal abuse
   • Emotionally destructive behavior

9. Unpleasant, loud • Cursing • Displacing anger to other sources
   • Expressing unrelated complaints • Verbal abuse
   • Emotionally destructive behavior

10. FOCUSING ANGER ON SOURCE • Unpleasant, loud • Cursing
    • Displacing anger to other sources • Throwing objects
    • Emotionally destructive behavior

11. Unpleasant, loud • Cursing • Displacing anger to other sources
    • Throwing objects • Emotionally destructive behavior

NEGATIVE

12. FOCUSING ANGER ON SOURCE • Unpleasant, loud • Cursing
    • Destroying property • Verbal abuse
    • Emotionally destructive behavior

13. Unpleasant, loud • Cursing • Displacing anger to other sources
    • Destroying property • Verbal abuse
    • Emotionally destructive behavior

14. Unpleasant, loud • Cursing • Displacing anger to other sources
    • Destroying property • Verbal abuse • Physical abuse
    • Emotionally destructive behavior

15. Passive-aggressive behavior

Note: Phrases in capital letters indicate positive ways to express anger feelings.
SOURCE: Ross Campbell, *How to Really Love Your Angry Child* (Colorado Springs: Cook, 2003).

this is true of your child, and now he is bringing verbal anger to you about a particular situation, this is exactly what you want to happen. For once your child has gotten the angry feelings out, you are then in an excellent position to train him.

When your child is speaking in anger, it does not necessarily mean that she is being disrespectful.

Isn't it unfair, you may wonder, *to expect me to feel thankful that my daughter is expressing the anger verbally and then to control myself?* We acknowledge this is not easy. But as you behave this way, you are forcing yourself to mature. And you are saving yourself and your family from some of life's worst problems later on. You may be wondering about children who verbalize anger most of the time, upset or not. It's true: some children express anger to manipulate their parents and get their own way, and that is unacceptable. Angry verbal expressions motivated by a desire to upset and hurt others are inappropriate and must be corrected. Handle those words like any misbehavior. But in the correction, practice the basic parental parameters: be kind but firm.

This may seem confusing, but letting your child bring his anger to you verbally when he is upset about a particular problem will provide you an opportunity to train him, as we will discuss below. Be sure to control yourself as your child expresses his anger verbally. And always remain kind but firm.

SEIZE THE MOMENT

After an angry outburst, seize the moment to help your child learn to handle her anger. As soon as things are stable between you, sit down together and do three things. Each will help your child deal with her anger in a positive way.

1. Let her know that you are not going to condemn her. Especially if a child is very responsive to authority, she may feel guilty about what she has done and never express her feelings again. Part of training is to let her know that you accept her as a person and always want to know how she is feeling, whether happy or sad or angry.

2. Commend your child for the things she did right. You may say, "You did let me know that you were angry, and that is good. You didn't let your anger out on your little brother or the dog. You didn't throw anything or hit the wall. You simply told me that you were angry." Mention whatever she did that was right. Anytime a child brings verbal anger to you, she has done some right things and avoided some wrong ones.

3. Help your child take a step up the Anger Ladder. The goal is to move your son or daughter toward a more positive anger response. So you want to give your child a request rather than a prohibition. Instead of saying, "Don't ever call me that name again!" you say, "From now on, Son, please don't call me that name. All right?" Of course, this doesn't guarantee that he will never again say what you have asked him not to. But it does ensure that when he is sufficiently mature, he will take that step. That may be the next day or several weeks or months down the road.

This kind of training is a long and difficult process, but, after you have done it enough times, your child will begin to do right without your reminder. The combination of your training, plus your good example of handling anger in a mature fashion, will help your child do her own self-training after a while.

For more information on helping children to handle anger, we recommend two books by Ross: *How to Really Love Your Child* and *How to Really Love Your Teenager.*

LOVE AND ANGER

Again, the most crucial element in training your children to manage their anger is your unconditional love for them. When they know that they are loved in this way, when they truly feel loved all the time, they will be far more responsive to your training. Also, you will be much more likely to achieve your goal of bringing them to emotional maturity by age seventeen.

We define love as looking out for another person's interests and seeking to meet her needs. With this definition, all wrongful words and deeds are actually a lack of love. We cannot be loving a child and at the same time be treating her poorly. To insist that we are still loving her when we are behaving badly toward her is to make the word *love* meaningless. A child treated this way does not feel loved. Rather, she feels angry, because she thinks that she is unloved.

We all know adults who are angry because they felt unloved by their parents. They may give very valid reasons for their anger, but at the root of those specifics is a lack of love. Their conclusion is, "If they loved me, they would not have treated me the way they did."

We are not suggesting that children who receive unconditional love, spoken in the primary and other love languages, will never get angry. They will, simply because we live in an imperfect world. Nor are we saying that in order to resolve your children's anger you must agree with their viewpoint. However, you must hear their viewpoint and come to understand their concern. Then you can judge whether they were wronged or misunderstood. At times you may need to apologize to your children. At other times, you may need to explain your reasoning for a decision you have made about their best interests. Even if they do not like your decision, they will respect it if you have taken time to fully hear and understand their complaints.

Processing anger and then training your children to deal with it in a mature way is one of the hardest parts of parenting. But the rewards are great. Speak your child's love language, keep his love tank filled, and watch him develop into a loving and responsible adult who knows how to process anger and helps other people do the same.

Speaking the Love Languages in Single-Parent Families

Filling a child's love tank can seem difficult at times: you are tired, your child is demanding, and you may feel that you need love yourself. At least you have your spouse to help you. Or do you?

In millions of single-parent homes, the answer is no. Instead of two parents filling a child's emotional tank on a regular basis, one does it alone. Instead of two parents giving love that flows through their marriage relationship, the love now is coming from a single mother or father who is wounded and lonely and pressured and without sufficient adult nurture.

Yet you can still speak your child's love language, filling his love tank. Everything we have said about loving your children is true, whether they reside with one parent or two. Single-parent families face many added issues, yet the power of the five love languages is no less. We emphasize this, realizing that single-parent households comprise 29.5 percent of all households with children, according to

2009 US Census statistics.[1] Because so many children are living in single-parent homes, we feel compelled to address some of the special needs of these families, including how to practice the love languages with your children.

We realize one-parent homes are not all equal. Some were created by divorce and others by the death of a spouse. Some parents have never married—in 2008 40.6 percent of all children were born to unmarried parents.[2] In those one-parent homes that resulted from divorce, some of the children have an ongoing positive contact with the noncustodial parent, while others suffer from a negative contact or total lack of relationship. Some single-parent families live near relatives and enjoy the benefit of closeness to grandparents, aunts and uncles, and cousins. Many others live far away from relatives and have to pretty much fend for themselves.

No matter what your situation, if you are a parent raising your children alone, we know you can effectively show love to your family, particularly by speaking your children's primary love language.

WHEN IT'S ALL UP TO YOU

The single mother or father trying to meet the needs of children while at the same time maintaining a career and some semblance of a personal life knows the tensions on the home front. If this is your situation, you know all too well the time pressures, the economic demands, and the social and personal changes you and your children have experienced. You know the doubts about whether you can do an adequate job of parenting. You have heard all the judgments from supposed experts about the pitfalls awaiting your children. At times, you feel the loneliness and exhaustion of having to do everything yourself.

Most single-parent homes today are the result of divorce, and research continues to show that divorce can be traumatic for children, especially when the divorce is not handled well by the two parents.

When a parent dies, the child knows that there was no choice. Usually the death was preceded by an illness, and this helped the child to understand death. Divorce is a choice on the part of one or both parents, even when that "choice" does seem to be a necessity. A parent who has been widowed will have to deal with a child's memories, but not with the quality of an ongoing helpful or hurtful connection with the one who is gone. A parent who has been divorced faces years of decisions in relationship to the noncustodial parent.

It would be hard to name another change that has more deeply affected the nature of our society today than divorce. Yet the increasing number of single-parent families created through divorce is a many-layered social problem beyond the scope of this book. Our focus is on what to do now: How can we help the children who find themselves in circumstances they never chose and cannot change? Our concern is also for the millions of single parents who are valiantly working to keep their families intact and to raise happy and responsible children.

HEALING THE WOUNDED

The needs of children in such homes are the same as of children from intact families. It is the *way* that these needs are met that changes; one parent is the primary caregiver instead of two. And the caregiver, whether single through divorce, death, or never being married, is usually wounded. Wounded parents are trying to minister to their wounded children and at the same time hoping to convince them that life can be fairly normal. Instead of the children having to cope with just the ordinary challenges of growing up, they now take on another whole set of concerns that ideally should not be part of their world.

Judith Wallerstein, founder of the Center for the Family in Transition, has done the most extensive research about the effects of divorce upon children. In her book *Second Chances: Men, Women, and Children a Decade after Divorce*,[3] she indicates that she entered her research with the notion commonly held among many adults: Divorce brings short-term pain, but eventually it provides greater happiness and fulfillment for everyone involved.

Wallerstein's years of research found that this assumption is not true. In many ways, children never get over the pain of divorce.

Most of the children whom Wallerstein, Sandra Blakeslee, and their associates interviewed saw themselves as being in a special category, "Children of Divorce." They felt a bond with others who had gone through the same experiences. The most common emotions of these children were fear, anger, and anxiety. As long as ten years after the parents divorced, these feelings still frequently surfaced.

HELPING YOUR CHILD THROUGH THE GRIEF

Such feelings can readily drain love from a child's emotional tank. As you speak your child's primary love language in order to refill her tank, be aware much love is needed. Denial, anger, then bargaining, and more anger—these are common responses to grief, which is felt by both children of divorce and those who have experienced the death of a parent. Eventually children find some level of acceptance to the loss of one parent. Some children can move through these stages of grieving more quickly if significant adults in their lives seek to openly communicate with them about their loss. They need someone to talk with and cry with. If family members cannot be involved in a helpful way, then a sympathetic pastor, friend, or counselor may fill this role.

Let's consider each of the responses and how parents and other adult friends can help the child move toward acceptance. Significantly, speaking the child's primary love language along the way will help the child in processing his grief.

Denial

Typically, the first response is *denial.* No child wants to believe that his parents are splitting up, or that one parent has died. He will talk as if his parents are simply separated for a season, or that the deceased parent is on a journey and will soon return. In this stage, the child is very frightened and feels a profound sense of sadness and loss. He may cry often from his intense longing that his parents be reunited. In the case of divorce, he may also sense that he is rejected.

Anger

The denial stage is accompanied and followed by intense *anger.* The child is angry at the parents for violating the unwritten rules of parenthood: Parents are supposed to care for their children, not abandon them. This anger may be expressed openly in words or may be held inside, for fear of upsetting the parents or fear of being punished for angry words and behavior. A child who is openly angry may have temper tantrums, verbal explosions, and may even be physically destructive. The child feels powerless—she has no say in what is happening to her. She also has a sense of profound loneliness and feels unable to talk with anyone.

The child's anger may be directed at the parent who left or at the custodial parent or both. In the case of death, the anger may be directed toward God. The child intensely needs to feel loved, to know that someone really cares. He is not likely to receive this from the parent who left. The child may or may not receive meaningful love from the custodial parent. And if a child believes that the parent who is present bears responsibility for the divorce, he may not be open to loving expressions from either parent. For that reason, grandparents and other family members, teachers, and religious leaders need to be sensitive to their opportunity to significantly meet the child's need for love. If they are aware of the child's primary love language, their efforts at meeting his emotional needs will be more effective.

Robbie's love language was physical touch. His father left when he was nine years old. Looking back, Robbie says, "If it had not been for my granddaddy, I'm not sure I would have made it. The first time I saw him after my father left, he took me in his arms and held me for a long time. He didn't say anything, but I knew he loved me and would always be there for me. Every time he came to see me, he hugged me and when he left, he did the same thing. I don't know if he knew how much the hugs meant to me, but they were like rain in the desert for me.

"My mom helped a lot by letting me talk and by asking me questions and encouraging me to share my pain. I knew she loved me, but in the early stages, I wasn't willing to receive her love," Robbie admitted. "She would try to hug me and I'd push her away. I think I blamed her for my father leaving. It wasn't until I found out that he left for another woman that I realized how I had misjudged her. Then I started receiving her hugs and we became close again."

Bargaining

Denial and anger are followed by *bargaining*. When parents separate, the child will make every effort to bring them back together. This may involve talking with the parents separately and together, pleading for them to work out their differences and reestablish the family unit. If verbal bargaining doesn't work, the child may subconsciously try manipulation by misbehaving in radical ways to get her parents' attention. She may also be testing the parents to see if they really care about her well-being. Her response could be drug use, petty theft, vandalism, sexual activity, or even suicide.

> Children who are overwhelmed with negative feelings have a hard time thinking clearly.

More Anger

Following bargaining will be *more anger.* In the hearts of children whose parents divorce, anger runs deep and lingers long. For at least a year after the divorce, they will probably struggle with emotions of guilt, anger, fear, and insecurity. Channeling so much energy into these feelings may result in lower grades at school, more aggressive negative social behavior, lessened respect for all adults, and intense loneliness. It is within such a painful setting that single parents seek to meet their children's need for love and at the same time establish some semblance of normalcy to the home. Theirs is not an easy task.

Wallerstein wrote: "After divorce you walk alone. All you've got is you. And it's scary." At the same time, "Little children need you more often . . . They are jittery and moody, and more clinging . . . Raising children always requires more time than you expected. They have more crises than you ever dreamed of. They demand sacrifice of time, money, hours spent at adult work and play."[4]

Learning to fill your child's love tank while your own is running low may seem difficult. But, like Robbie's mother, the wise parent will come to understand what her child uniquely needs—and seek to meet that need.

HOW STORIES HELP

Children who are overwhelmed with negative feelings have a hard time thinking clearly. If you are the single parent of such children, reading together can help your children begin to think clearly about their pain and loss. You will want to have a storybook they can understand. Select stories, songs, and poems appropriate to the ages of your children, through the early teen years. This can be a warm, bonding time. Many enjoyable stories have strong ethical and moral lessons, such as "Pinocchio" and stories by Beatrix Potter. There are several guides to help you choose good literature. We recommend *Honey for a Child's Heart*, by Gladys Hunt; *Books That Build Character*, by William Kilpatrick; and *The Book of Virtues*, by William Bennett.

Be alert to your child's reactions as you read to her. Ask what she is thinking to open opportunities for discussion at her level. If you are reading about a child or animal that is lost and your child expresses concern, you have a great opportunity to praise her for her caring heart. You can also talk about what it feels like to be lost, or to lose someone dear to you.

Children also need help in playing the blame game. Anger can confuse their thinking. It is not uncommon for them to believe that blaming other people is justified, simply because they feel angry. When they are calm, you can explain different sides of a situation, not only about other children but also about what has happened in your family. Especially when children feel terribly wronged by a parent they think has abandoned them, they need to know that their sense of loss is natural and nothing to feel guilty about.

And, as you read together, you can talk about what is happening in your children's daily lives. You can also make up stories together. This will help you to understand what is going on inside your children, at levels they may be unable to articulate in discussion.

ASK FOR HELP!

No parent can single-handedly meet a child's need for love. As we said before, some children may choose not to accept love from either parent; their hurt and anger are so great that they will not allow the possibility of love. This is where grandparents and other extended family members, as well as church and community resources, come into play.

If you are a single parent, don't wait until people ask if they can help. Some may be holding back, not wanting to interfere in your family. Others may not be aware of your situation. If you or your children need help, you may want to investigate the resources available in your community. Someone at your children's school or your church can guide you in your search.

Extended family members are always important, but they become even more crucial when children suffer losses. For instance, nearby grandparents can help the grandchildren in several ways during the school week, and their presence can cheer their own single-parent son or daughter. They may be able to come over and help the children get ready for school in the morning or help chauffeur in the afternoon. They also take some of the emotional burden off the single parent.

There are many people who would be glad to help single-parent families if they know that their help is needed. They want to feel useful, and you need some help. The only problem is getting these two together. A local church is a good place to make this happen, and some churches are networking in just such a way. If you find it difficult to make your needs known, just remember that you are doing this not primarily for yourself but for the well-being of your children.

LOVE LANGUAGES IN THE SINGLE-PARENT HOUSEHOLD

A child's need for emotional love is just as important after the divorce as it was before. The difference is that the child's love tank has been ruptured by the severe trauma of divorce. The love tank will have to be repaired by hours of sympathetic listening and processing of the emotions we have talked about. Someone must nurture the child through the grief process if that child is ever again to believe that he or she is truly loved. The process of repairing the love tank is itself an expression of love. Listening much, talking less, helping your child face reality, acknowledging hurt, and empathizing with pain are all part of it.

Of course, the primary way to refill the love tank is to speak your child's love language. Keep in mind that the child's primary love language does not change simply because the parents have separated due to divorce or death. Learn your child's love language and then tell the significant adults in your child's life what the child's primary love language is.

In the early weeks following a divorce, when a child may be unable to receive love from either parent, other significant adults may be the only ones able to express love to the child. If your child receives love primarily through affirming words, he may well receive them from grandparents or other adults yet temporarily reject them from you. A child whose primary love language is gifts may actually throw a gift back in the face of a parent recently divorced. Do not be angered by this but realize the behavior is part of your child's grieving process. Once the child has reached the acceptance stage and understands that he cannot put his parents' marriage back together, and that he is going to be living in a single-parent home, he may perhaps receive love on an emotional level from both parents.

If children receive the right kinds of love at times when they especially need it, they can come through the pains of family separation intact and go on to satisfying adult lives. One example of this is Bob Kobielush, president of the Christian Camping Foundation. Bob's father was a successful businessman and his mother was a homemaker. When Bob was young, his father gave up his business to join a cult, moving the family of five boys several times. When his father became ill with polio and was completely disabled, the family returned to their home state of Wisconsin to be near extended family. When Bob was nine, his parents divorced.

About this time, Bob and his brothers came under Christian influence and they all received Christ as their Savior. With no means of support, their mother was forced to go on welfare until she was able to get enough odd jobs. She later finished her academic preparation and became a teacher.

Today Bob and his brothers are all happily married, well educated, and productive. Bob says, "Mom always majored on the majors in positive ways. She didn't talk about the negative things. It seemed as if we were a normal family. I didn't know we weren't. I don't know how we would have turned out without a godly mother and extended family to model the practical Christian life. I thank God for my background and for my single mom."

> Keep up your hope and hold on to your dreams for your children.

Archibald Hart, dean emeritus of the School of Psychology at Fuller Seminary in California, credits the power of family and God for his growing strong in a single-parent home. Originally from South Africa, the Hart family broke up after years of conflict. Archibald's mother seemed happier after the divorce, but economic worries compelled her to send Archibald and his brother to live with their grandparents. They were a strong Christian influence, motivating the boys by saying, "There is nothing you can't do."

Hart gives this advice to single parents: "Nothing is unchangeable. If you have no support network now, build it, and you will be amazed at how many will respond. Your children can become more resilient, productive, and creative if the circumstances are right. A life that is too easy is not good for the soul."[5]

Keep up your hope and hold on to your dreams for your children. While things may seem rough now, there is another day, another year. If you and the children are making steady progress away from the sense of loss, if you are all growing in the many areas of life, you can feel assured that the growth will continue. It has become a pattern, a habit that will not easily be forgotten.

MEETING YOUR OWN NEED FOR LOVE

While we have talked primarily about the child whose parents have divorced, we are keenly aware that the single parent seeking to meet the child's needs is also a creature of need. While the child is working through the emotions of guilt, fear, anger, and insecurity, one or both parents are also working through similar emotions. The mother who has been abandoned by a husband may have found a new male interest; the mother who forced a physically abusive spouse to leave now struggles with her own feelings of rejection and loneliness. A single parent's emotional need for love is just as real as anyone else's need. Because that need cannot be met by the former spouse or by the child, the single parent often reaches out to friends. This is an effective way to begin to have your love tank filled.

A word of caution as you make new friends. The single parent at this point is extremely vulnerable to members of the opposite sex who may take advantage in a time of weakness. Because the single parent so desperately needs love, there is grave danger of accepting that love from someone who will take advantage sexually, financially, or emotionally. It is extremely important that the newly single parent be very selective in making new friends. The safest source for love is from long-term friends who know members of the extended family. A single parent who tries to satisfy the need for love in an irresponsible manner can end up with tragedy upon tragedy.

With your children, you have a tremendous resource of love. For deep down they do love you. And they need your love. As psychologists Sherill and Prudence Tippins say, "The best gift you can give your child is your own emotional, physical, spiritual, and intellectual health."[6] As painful as it may seem, the truth is that you may be a single parent for many years. During this time, long or short, you will want to give your children the example of integrity and responsibility that can be a model for them in their journey to responsible adulthood.

Speaking the Love Languages in Marriage

S omeone has said, "The best way to love your children is to love their mother [father]." That's true. The quality of your marriage greatly affects the way you relate to your children—and the way they receive love. If your marriage is healthy—both partners treating each other with kindness, respect, and integrity—you and your spouse will feel and act as partners in parenting. But if you are critical, harsh, and unloving toward each other, you are not likely to be in accord as you raise your children. And the children, always sensitive to feelings, will sense it.

It's probably obvious now: the most essential emotional element in a happy and healthy marriage is love. Just as your child has an emotional love tank, you do too. And so does your spouse. We want to feel deeply loved by our mates, for then the world looks bright. But when the love tank is empty, we have the gnawing feeling, "My spouse doesn't really love me," and our whole world begins to look dark. Much of the straying and misbehavior in marriages grow out of these empty love tanks.

To feel loved and to strengthen your child's sense of being loved, you need to speak your spouse's primary love language as well. We conclude *The 5 Love Languages of Children* by talking about the love languages of adults. As a husband or wife, you will find that one of the five love languages speaks more deeply to you emotionally than the others. When your spouse expresses love to you in this primary language, you really feel loved. You like all five languages, but this one is special.

Much of the straying and misbehavior in marriage grow out of empty love tanks.

As children differ, so do adults. Seldom do a husband and wife have the same primary love language. Don't assume your spouse speaks your language or a language you learned from your parents. Those are two common mistakes. Maybe your father said, "Son, always give a woman flowers. Nothing is more important than flowers." And so you give your wife flowers and it seems to be no big deal to her. The problem is not in your sincerity but that you are not speaking her primary language. She appreciates the flowers, but one of the other languages would speak more deeply to her.

If spouses do not speak each other's primary language, their love tanks will not be filled; when they come down off the "in love" emotional high, their differences will seem bigger and their frustration with each other will mount. They may think about the warm emotions they used to experience and seek to recapture that "in love" feeling so they will be happy again. And yet, they don't know how to do it with their spouse, since life at home has become dull and predictable and far less than satisfying.

"IN LOVE" OR LOVING?

Too many people enter marriage through a "falling in love" experience, during which they see the object of their love as perfect. While they are blind to any imperfections, they are also sure that their experience of love is unique and that they are the first to love anyone so deeply. Of course, in time their eyes are opened and they come down to earth where they can see the other person as he or she really is, warts and all. The vast majority of "in love" experiences end up "out of love."

Most people have fallen in love, maybe several times, and they look back on those experiences with thanksgiving that they didn't do anything foolish while the sensation was at its peak. But too many people today are acting on the obsession and causing great harm to their families. That's how marital affairs begin, seeking after an elusive feeling they may have had during their dating years or early months of marriage. But lesser feelings do not mean dwindling love.

There is a difference between love and being "in love." The "in love" feeling is temporary, a primitive emotional reaction that often has little logical basis. Genuine love is quite different, in that it places the needs of the other person first and desires for the partner to grow and flourish. Genuine love allows the mate to choose to return the love. In marriage, we all need a partner who will choose to love us. When that happens, we can happily receive love from the other one and feel thrilled that our mate benefits from our efforts to love and make him or her happy.

This kind of love takes sacrifice and hard work. Most couples reach a point where they lose those exhilarating "in love" feelings and wonder if they still love the one they married. It is then that they need to decide whether they are going to make their marriage work, to care for their mate regardless of everything else, or if they are just going to let the relationship go.

You may find yourself thinking, "But this sounds so sterile. Love as an 'attitude' with appropriate behavior?" As I mentioned in the book *The 5 Love Languages,* some spouses really like and desire the fireworks.

Where are the shooting stars, the balloons, the deep emotions? What about the spirit of anticipation, the twinkle in the eye, the electricity in a kiss, the excitement of sex? What about the emotional security of knowing that I am number one in my partner's thoughts?[1]

That's not wrong, of course. Such feelings at times reward our commitment to relationship. But we shouldn't expect them. Yet we do need our mate to fill our love tank. He will do it if he speaks the love language we understand.

That's what Carla was missing in her marriage. "I just don't feel that Rick loves me anymore," she told her sister one day. "Our relationship is empty and I feel so alone. I used to be number one in Rick's life, but now I rank about twenty—after his job, golf, football, Scouts, his family, the car, and just about everything else. I think he is glad that I'm here, doing my part, but he takes me for granted. Oh, he gets me nice gifts on Mother's Day, my birthday, and our anniversary, and he sends me flowers on all the right days, but the gifts seem empty.

"Rick never has any time for me. We don't go anywhere together, never do anything as a couple, and hardly talk anymore. I get angry just thinking about it. I used to beg him to spend time with me, and he said I was criticizing him. He told me to get off his back and leave him alone. He said I should be thankful that he has a good job, isn't on drugs, and doesn't run around on me. Well, excuse me, but that's not enough. I want a husband who loves me and acts as if I am important enough to spend time with."

Do you spot the love language Carla understands best, that Rick does not speak? Rick is speaking the language of gifts; Carla is crying for quality time. In the early years, she received his gifts as expressions of love; but because he ignored her primary love language, her love tank is now empty and his gifts no longer count for much.

If Carla and Rick can discover each other's primary love language and learn to speak it, the emotional warmth of love can return to their marriage. No, not the obsessive, irrational euphoria of the "in love" experience, but something far more important—a deep inner feeling of being loved by their spouse. They will know that they are number one to the other; that they respect, admire, and appreciate each other as persons, and want to be together, living in an intimate partnership.

This is the kind of marriage people dream of, and it can be a reality when couples learn to speak each other's primary love language on a regular basis. And it will make them stronger parents, working more as a team while giving the children security and a greater sense of love. Let's look at how this can play out with each of the love languages.

WORDS OF AFFIRMATION

"I work hard," Mark said, "and I've been fairly successful in my business. I'm a good father and, in my opinion, a good husband. All I ever expect from my wife is a little appreciation, but instead, what I get is criticism. It doesn't matter how hard I work or what I do, it is never enough. Jane is always after me about something. I just don't understand it. Most women would be glad to have a husband like me. Why is she so critical?"

As frantically as he can, Mark is waving a banner that reads, "My love language is words of affirmation. Will somebody please love me?"

But Jane doesn't know about the five love languages any more than Mark does.[2] She can't see his banner and hasn't the foggiest idea why he feels unloved. She reasons, "I'm a good homemaker. I take care of the kids, work full-time, and keep myself looking attractive. What more could he want? Most men would be happy to come home to a good meal and a clean house."

Jane probably doesn't even know that Mark feels unloved. She simply knows that periodically he explodes and tells her to stop being critical of him. If he were asked, Mark would probably admit that he enjoys the good meals and appreciates a clean house, but these do not meet his emotional need for love. His primary language is words of affirmation, and without such words, his love tank will never be full.

To the spouse whose primary love language is words of affirmation, spoken or written expressions of appreciation are like rain falling on a spring garden.

"I'm so proud of you and the way you handled the situation with Robert."

"This is a great meal. You deserve a place in the chef's hall of fame."

"The lawn really looks nice. Thanks for all your hard work."

"Ohhh, don't you look amazing tonight!"

"I haven't told you this in a long time, but I really appreciate that you work regularly and help pay the bills. I know it is hard on you sometimes, and I do thank you for your great contribution."

"I love you so much. You are the most wonderful husband/wife in the world!"

Affirming words may be written as well as spoken. Before we were married, many of us wrote love letters and poems. Why not continue or revive this expression of love after marriage? If you find writing difficult, buy a card and underline the words that express your feelings and perhaps add a brief note at the bottom of the card.

Speak words of affirmation in the presence of other family members or friends and you gain an extra benefit. Not only does your spouse feel loved, but you have given others an example of how to speak affirming words. Let her mother hear you brag about your wife, and you may have a fan for life!

If such words are sincerely spoken or written, they speak volumes to a person whose primary love language is words of affirmation.

QUALITY TIME

John wrote me after reading the book *The 5 Love Languages.* "For the first time I realized why Beth had complained so much about our not spending time together—her primary love language was quality time.

"Before, I had always accused her of being negative, of not appreciating all that I did for her," John wrote. "I'm a person of action—I like to clean up messes and get things organized. From the early days of our marriage, I have always been good at fixing things around the house, keeping the yard looking good. I never understood why Beth didn't seem to value all this but always complained that we didn't spend time together.

"When the lights came on in my mind, I realized that she really did appreciate those things, but that they didn't make her feel loved because service was not her love language. And so, the first thing I did was to plan a weekend away, just the two of us. We hadn't done that in several years. When she knew I was making the arrangements, she was like a kid going on a vacation."

After that special weekend, John looked at their finances and decided to have weekend getaways every couple of months. The weekend treks took them to different parts of their state. His letter continued:

"I also told her that I wanted us to spend fifteen minutes every night sharing with each other about the day. She thought this was great but could hardly believe I would initiate it.

"Since our first weekend away, Beth's attitude has been totally different. She expresses appreciation for all the things I do around the house. Also, she is no longer critical—yes, my primary love language is words of affirmation. We haven't felt this good in years. Our only regret is that we didn't discover the five love languages earlier in our marriage."

Beth and John's experience is similar to that of thousands of other couples when they discover each other's primary love language. Like John, we must both learn our spouse's primary love language and learn to speak that love language regularly. As you do so, the other four languages will have enhanced meaning, because your spouse's love tank will be kept full.

GIFTS

All human cultures incorporate gift-giving as an expression of love between husband and wife. This usually begins before marriage, whether during the dating phase as in Western cultures or during the period before a prearranged marriage. In the West, gift-giving has been emphasized more for the male than for the female, but the receiving of gifts may also be a primary love language of men. Many husbands have admitted that when their wives come home and show them the clothes they have bought for themselves, their silent thought is, "I wonder if she will ever think about getting me a shirt, tie, or pair of socks? Does she ever think of me when she is shopping?"

For spouses whose primary love language is receiving gifts, a present says, "He was thinking about me." Or, "Look what she bought for me." Most gifts require a good deal of thought, and it is this thought-fulness that communicates the love. We even say, "It is the thought that counts." However, it is not the thought left in your head that counts—the gifts actually should be presented.

You may be unsure what to give. If so, get help. When Rob discovered that his wife's primary love language was gifts, he was at a loss as to what to do because he didn't know how to buy gifts. And so he recruited his sister to go shopping with him once a week to buy his wife a gift. After three months of this, he was able to select his own presents.

Cindy's husband, Bill, enjoyed golf, and Cindy knew he would like something related to his hobby. But what? She had never learned much about the game. So twice a year she asked one of his golfing buddies to secure a golf-related gift which she in turn gave to Bill. He was always elated at how in tune she was with his desires.

Bart was a suit-and-tie man five days a week. Once a month his wife, Annie, visited the store where Bart bought his suits and asked the salesman to pick out a tie for him. The salesman kept a list of the suits, so that the ties always matched. Bart told everyone what a thoughtful wife Annie was.

Of course, buying a husband gifts assumes that the wife has available cash. If she does not work outside the home, this may mean that in a budget discussion with her husband, they should agree on a monthly amount from which she can buy gifts. If his primary love language is gifts, her husband will be happy to make that budget adjustment.

There is always a way to learn to speak your spouse's primary language. It may take some creativity, but there is no law that says you have to do things just like other people do. Make the gifts you select tie in with your spouse's hobby or some interest he or she is just beginning to explore. Or shop for a gift when you are away together for a day or more. You might buy a gift card for a restaurant you both like, or tickets to a play or concert. Or even a handmade certificate good for a certain amount of work to be done in the house or yard by you or by a professional. Or a couple of quiet days at a retreat center for a mother of young children. Your gift to your spouse could be a new sound system or work to be done on an older piano that he or she values.

ACTS OF SERVICE

Andy was livid as he talked with a counselor. "I don't understand it. Sarah said she wanted to be a full-time mom and that's fine with me, since I make enough money to support us. But if she is going to stay at home, I don't understand why she can't keep the house in decent order. When I come home in the evening, it's like walking into a disaster area. The bed is unmade. Her nightgown is still lying on the chair. Clean clothes are piled on top of the dryer, and the baby's toys are scattered all over. If she went shopping, the groceries are still in the bags. And she's watching TV, giving no thought to what we are going to have for supper.

"I'm sick of living in a pigpen. All I'm asking is that she keep the house in a halfway decent condition. She doesn't have to cook every night—we can go out a couple of times a week."

Andy's primary love language was acts of service and the gauge on his love tank was reading empty. He didn't care if Sarah stayed home or worked outside the home, but he wanted to live in a greater degree of order than they did. He felt that if she cared about him she would show it by having the house in better order and preparing meals several times a week.

By nature, Sarah was not an organized person. She was creative and enjoyed doing exciting things with the children. She placed the relationship with the children on a higher level of priority than keeping the house clean. Speaking Andy's primary love language, acts of service, seemed almost impossible to her.

Their story may help you understand why we use the metaphor of language. If you grew up speaking English, then learning German or Japanese could seem very difficult. In a similar way, learning to speak the language of acts of service can be difficult. But when you come to understand that service is your spouse's primary language, you can decide to find a way to speak it eloquently.

> **It is not difficult to find out what your spouse would most desire. Just think of what they have most complained about in the past.**

For Sarah, the answer was to work out an arrangement with a teenager next door to come over late in the afternoon to play with the children, so that Sarah could give the house a "Let's love Andy" treatment. In exchange for the childcare, she tutored the teenager in algebra several times a week. Also, Sarah began to consciously plan three dinner meals each week, preparing them in the morning and leaving only the finishing touches for evening.

Another wife in a similar situation decided, along with a friend, to take a course in basic meal preparation at a local technical institute. They cared for each other's children while they were in class and also enjoyed the stimulation of meeting new people in the class.

Doing something that you know your spouse would like is one of love's fundamental languages. Such acts as emptying the dishwasher, running to the drugstore to pick up a prescription, rearranging furniture, trimming shrubs, and cleaning the bathrooms are all ways of serving. It can be little things like straightening up papers in the home office or changing the baby's diaper. It is not difficult to find out what your spouse would most desire. Just think of what they have most complained about in the past. If you can do these acts of service as expressions of love, they will seem far more noble than if you think of them as humdrum tasks that have no special meaning.

PHYSICAL TOUCH

We must not equate physical touch simply with the sexual part of marriage. To be sure, lovemaking involves touch, but physical touch as an expression of love should not be limited to sexual intercourse. Putting your hand on your spouse's shoulder, running your hand through her hair, massaging his neck or back, touching her arm as you give her a cup of coffee—these are all expressions of love. Of course, love is also expressed by holding hands, kissing, embracing, sexual foreplay, and intercourse. For the spouse whose primary love language is physical touch, these are love's loudest voices.

"When my husband takes time to massage my back, I know he loves me. He is focusing on me. Every movement of his hands says, 'I love you.' I feel closest to him when he is touching me." Jill is clearly revealing her primary love language, physical touch. She may appreciate gifts, words of affirmation, quality time, and acts of service, but what most deeply communicates on an emotional level is her husband's physical touch. Without that, the words may seem empty, the gifts and time meaningless, and the acts of service as so much duty. But if she is receiving physical touch, her love tank will be full and the love expressed in other languages will cause it to overflow.

Because a man's sexual drive is physically based, whereas a woman's sexual desire is emotionally based, husbands often assume that their own primary love language is physical touch. This is particularly true for those whose sexual needs are not met regularly. As their desire for sexual release overpowers their need for emotional love, they think this is their deepest need. If, however, their sexual needs are met, they may well discern that physical touch is not their primary love language. One way to tell is how much they enjoy physical touch that is not associated with sexual intercourse. If this is not high on their list, physical touch is probably not their primary language.

DISCOVER AND SPEAK YOUR SPOUSE'S LOVE LANGUAGE

You may be asking, "Does this really work? Will it make a difference in our marriage?" The best way to find out is to try. If you don't know your spouse's primary love language, you could ask him or her to read this chapter and then you can talk about it. If your mate is not willing to read or to talk about it, you may have to guess. Think about his complaints, his requests, and his behavior. Also, the love language he speaks to you and others may give you a clue.

With that educated guess in mind, focus on the likely primary language and see what happens over the next few weeks. If you have judged correctly, you will probably see a change in the attitude and spirit of your spouse. If he asks why you are acting strangely, you can just say that you read something on love languages and are trying to be a better lover. The chances are good that your spouse will want to know more, and you may want to read *The 5 Love Languages* together, as well as this book.

Speak each other's primary love language regularly and you will see a profound difference in the emotional climate between the two of you. With full love tanks you are better able to fill your children's love tanks. We believe you will find your marriage and family life much more enjoyable.

Speak your spouse's primary love language; speak your children's love language. And as you find it making a difference, share the message of this book with your extended family and friends. Family by family, we can create a more loving society. What you do in loving your family will make a difference in our nation.

What Might Be Is Still Ahead

A s you recognize and begin to speak the primary love language of your child, we know the outcome will be a more solid family relationship and benefits for you and your children. As we said in chapter 1, speaking your child's love language won't end all problems, but it can bring stability to your home and hope to your child. It's a wonderful opportunity.

But you may have doubts and other concerns as you begin to speak a new love language, concerns about your past or your abilities in the present. Such concerns also represent opportunities. We now look at those special opportunities you have, no matter your past or present situation.

It would seem that the ideal reader for this book is a couple just starting a family or who have very young children. We know, however, that some of our readers have older children in the home or even adult children. You may be thinking, *If only I had read this book earlier . . . but it's sort of late now.* Many parents look back at the way they raised their family and realize that they didn't do a very good job of meeting their children's emotional needs. And now, those children may be grown and have families of their own.

If you are among those parents with regrets, you probably look back and ask why things went wrong. Maybe your work took you away from home too much in those critical child-rearing years. Or perhaps it was your own turbulent childhood that left you so unequipped to be a parent. You may have lived all your life with an empty love tank so that you never learned how to speak love to your children.

Even though you have learned a lot since those years, you may have concluded, "What happened, happened, and there's not much we can do about it now." We would like to suggest another possibility, "What might be is still ahead." The opportunities are still there. The wonderful thing about human relationships is that they are not static. The potential for making them better is always present.

Developing a closer relationship with your teenage or adult children may require tearing down walls and building bridges—some very hard but rewarding work. Maybe it is time to admit to your children what you have already admitted to yourself—that you did not do a very good job of communicating love on an emotional level. If they are still in your home or live nearby, you can do this face-to-face, looking into their eyes and asking their forgiveness. Or you may need to write this in a letter, making a sincere apology and expressing a hope for a more positive relationship in the future. You can't undo the past, but you can forge a different kind of future.

Perhaps you were not only poor communicators, but you actually abused your children, emotionally, physically, or sexually. Perhaps alcohol or other drugs were your cohorts in crime, or maybe your own pain and immaturity rendered you victims to your anger. Whatever your failure, it is never too late to tear down the walls. You can never build bridges until you get rid of the walls. (If you are still abusing your children, you likely will need a trained counselor to help you break this destructive pattern.)

The most positive thing to do with a past failure is to confess it and ask forgiveness. You cannot erase the deeds any more than you can erase all their results. But you can experience emotional and spiritual cleansing through confession and the possibility of forgiveness. Whether or not your children verbally express forgiveness, the fact that you have been mature enough to admit your failures gives them a bit more respect for you. In time, they may be open to your efforts to build bridges. And who knows, the day may come when they allow you the privilege of a closer relationship with them—and their children.

Even if you were not the parent you wish you had been, you can begin now to love your children in ways that will make them feel truly valued. And as they have children, you will know that you are influencing another generation of your family, those little ones who now will have a better chance at receiving unconditional love all their days.

With full love tanks, your grandchildren will be more receptive and active intellectually, socially, spiritually, and relationally than they would be without this. When children feel genuinely loved, their whole world looks brighter. Their inner spirit is more secure and they are far more likely to reach their potential for good in the world.

I (Gary) dream of a day when all children can grow up in homes filled with love and security, where their developing energies can be channeled to learning and serving rather than craving and searching for the love they did not receive at home. It is my desire that this book will help this dream to become a reality for many children.

Gary has mentioned the opportunity of emotional and spiritual cleansing through forgiveness. I (Ross) encourage you to remember the spiritual dimension of parenting. The greatest source of encouragement I have found in my own parenting is the promises of God. My wife, Pat, and I have had many difficult bridges to cross, including the birth of a profoundly retarded daughter, and we can assure you that God is always near, ready to help and honor each of His wonderful promises. My favorite promises for parents are in Psalm 37:25–26.

I was young and now I am old,
yet I have never seen the righteous forsaken
or their children begging bread.
They are always generous and lend freely;
their children will be a blessing.

I have stood on those two Scripture verses for many years and have tested those promises countless times. I have never seen the righteous forsaken. And I have seen the children of the righteous blessed and becoming a blessing.

As I have seen my children grow and mature in every way, I have been heartened not only that God is keeping His promises and blessing my children but that I am truly His child also. Pat and I have gone through many trials in which we had real difficulty seeing our way, but God always came through and brought us out of them.

I want to encourage you in your parenting. No matter what your situation is now or will be in the future, God will never forsake you. He will always be there for you and see you through to the end. As you raise your children, there are opportunities to develop the spiritual aspects of their lives—and your own.

The Old Testament prophet Isaiah, declaring God's words, wrote:

Fear not, for I am with you;
Be not dismayed, for I am your God.
I will strengthen you,
Yes, I will help you,
I will uphold you with My righteous right hand.[1]

Such a verse can carry you through some rough periods in life and in parenting; that verse certainly has sustained Pat and me. Without God's assurances and promises, I know our story would be quite different than it has been.

The psalmist calls children "a gift of the Lord," a "reward," a "heritage."[2] Children are the most wonderful gift we can have. If they mean so much to God, they should mean everything to us, their parents. I would like to suggest that you make a list of "requirements" for being a good parent. Don't let the word *requirement* put pressure or guilt on you as a caring parent. These "requirements" should help you feel good about your authority and role as a parent. Relax and really enjoy your children.

When I was a fledgling dad, I found myself worrying; I was insecure in my parenting. But then I discovered that once a parent understands what a child needs, it is not that difficult to meet those "requirements." The best news is that almost any caring parent is able to do this.

I urge you to make up your own requirement list. Start with a few items and then add to the list as you want to. When you see that you are meeting those requirements, you can be assured that your child is receiving good parenting, and you can relax and enjoy your child. It would be hard to describe to you how much this assurance has helped me. In fact, I soon found that I was a better parent than I ever thought I could be.

Most of the "requirements" for good parenting are in this book. If you want to make a list, I can give you a start. But the list won't be complete or be yours until you frame it in your own thoughts and words. Here is my personal list, my own "Requirements to Be a Good Parent":

1 Keep my child's emotional love tank full—speak the five love languages.

2 Use the most positive ways I can to control my child's behavior: requests, gentle physical manipulation, commands, punishment, and behavior modification.

3 Lovingly discipline my child. Ask, "What does this child need?" and then go about it logically.

4 Do my best to handle my own anger appropriately and not dump it on my child. Be kind but firm.

5 Do my best to train my child to handle anger maturely.

I hope you will make your own requirement list soon. As you realize that you are able to do what you have written on your list, you will be able to relax and enjoy your children. And they will become increasingly secure in every way.

A study guide, with questions and exercises
for parents and groups, is available online at
www.5lovelanguages.com

Notes

Chapter 1: Love Is the Foundation

1. Lori Gottlieb, "How to Land Your Kid in Therapy," *Atlantic*, July/August 2011, 64–78.

Chapter 2: Love Language #1: Physical Touch

1. Mark 10:13 NKJV.
2. Mark 10:14–16 NIV.

Chapter 3: Love Language #2: Words of Affirmation

1. Proverbs 18:21 NIV.
2. Proverbs 15:1 NIV.
3. Helen P. Mrosla, "All the Good Things," *Reader's Digest*, October 1991, 49–52.

Chapter 4: Love Language #3: Quality Time

1. Sandy Dengler, *Susanna Wesley* (Chicago: Moody, 1987), 171.

Chapter 6: Love Language #5: Acts of Service

1. Luke 14:12–14 NIV.

Chapter 9: Learning and the Love Languages

1. Burton L. White, *The Origins of Human Competence* (Lexington, MA: D. C. Heath and Company, 1979), 31.

Chapter 11: Speaking the Love Languages in Single-Parent Families

1. Research from *census.gov*.

2. Ibid.

3. Judith Wallerstein and Sandra Blakeslee, *Second Chances: Men, Women, and Children a Decade after Divorce* (New York: Ticknor & Fields, 1990).

4. Judith Wallerstein, "Parenting after Divorce: What Really Happens and Why," *huffingtonpost.com*, November 29, 2010.

5. Lynda Hunter, "Wings to Soar," *Single Parent Family*, May 1996, 7.

6. Sherill and Prudence Tippins, *Two of Us Make a World* (New York: Henry Holt, 1995), 56.

Chapter 12: Speaking the Love Languages in Marriage

1. Gary Chapman, *The 5 Love Languages* (Chicago: Northfield, 2015), 37.

2. If after reading this chapter you feel you need to learn more about spotting your spouse's primary love language and practicing that language, read *The 5 Love Languages*. It's written specifically for married and engaged couples.

Epilogue: What Might Be Is Still Ahead

1. Isaiah 41:10 NKJV.

2. Psalm 127:3; see New American Standard Bible, New King James Version, and New International Version.

More Helps for Parents

Ross Campbell, *How to Really Love Your Child*. Colorado Springs: Cook, 2004.

Ross Campbell, *How to Really Love Your Angry Child*. Colorado Springs: Cook, 2003.

Les Carter and Frank Minirth, *The Anger Workbook*. New York: Wiley & Sons, 2004.

Gary Chapman, *The 5 Love Languages*. Chicago: Northfield, 2015.

Gary Chapman, *The Family You've Always Wanted*. Chicago: Northfield, 2008.

Foster W. Cline and Jim Fay, *Parenting with Love and Logic*. Colorado Springs: NavPress, 2006.

Mary DeMuth, *You Can Raise Courageous and Confident Kids*. Eugene, Oreg.: Harvest House, 2011.

focusonthefamily.com: This website is packed with helpful resources on a wide variety of family-oriented topics.

John Fuller, *First-Time Dad*. Chicago: Moody, 2011.

Willard F. Harley, *Mom's Needs, Dad's Needs: Keeping Romance Alive Even after the Kids Arrive.* Grand Rapids: Revell, 2003.

Tim Kimmel, *Grace-Based Parenting.* Nashville: Thomas Nelson, 2005.

Kathy Koch, PhD, *8 Great Smarts: Discover and Nurture Your Child's Intelligences.* Chicago: Moody, 2016.

Kevin Leman, *Have a New Kid by Friday.* Grand Rapids: Revell, 2008.

Kevin Leman, *Single Parenting That Works.* Grand Rapids: Revell, 2006.

James R. Lucas, *1001 Ways to Connect with Your Kids.* Wheaton, Ill.: Tyndale, 2000.

Arlene Pellicane, *Growing Up Social: Raising Relational Kids in a Screen-Driven World.* Chicago: Moody, 2014.

John Rosemond, *Parenting by the Book.* New York: Howard, 2007.

Jill Savage and Kathy Koch, PhD, *No More Perfect Kids: Love Your Kids for Who They Are.* Chicago: Moody, 2014.

Tedd Tripp, *Shepherding a Child's Heart.* Wapwallopen, Pa.: Shepherd Press, 1995.

H. Norman Wright, *Helping Your Kids Deal with Anger, Fear, and Sadness.* Eugene, Oreg.: Harvest, 2005.

For Parents and Kids:

THE LOVE LANGUAGES MYSTERY GAME

FOR PARENTS OF CHILDREN 5 TO 8 YEARS OLD:

So many parents wonder about their child's love language, and admittedly, determining the love language of a young child requires some educated guesswork. Why? Because young children can't yet verbalize their love language. However, for children ages 5 to 8 years old, you might try the following exercise. Ask him or her to draw or call out some ways parents love their children. You should try not to guide their drawings or answers, limit their responses, or require more responses than what he or she is prepared to give at the time you ask. Depending on the child's attention span and the time of day, you may get many answers, or you may get very few. If it seems like slow going, then you may want to secretly explore the subject of love with your child for a week or so until you can deduce what he or she perceives as love.

You may find yourself reading books or watching TV or a movie with your child and asking the question, "How do you know that mommy or daddy loves that little boy or little girl?" Or you may intentionally experiment by expressing love in each of the five ways over a week's period of time. This will be a subjective measure, but the combination of all these suggestions—studying your child's answers or drawings, listening to his or her answers about other parents and children, and "measuring" his or her response to your expression of each of the five love languages—should be enough to help you accurately assess your child's primary love language. If you are lucky enough to catch your child in a talkative or expressive mood, you may be able to get him or her to identify several ways parents show love. You'll be looking for a theme or a repetition in their answers, and from this, you can accurately determine your child's love language.

FOR PARENTS OF CHILDREN 9 TO 12:

By the time a child is 9 years old, he or she is better able to identify and express his or her feelings about love than when he or she was younger. Parents still have to keep in mind that children this age have a limited attention for and limited interest in such things as helping you determine their love language. The following "game" should help you in your research.

Tell your child you would like help solving "The Love Language Mystery Game." Explain that you need him or her to look at a list of "clues" and that these clues are comments that parents sometimes make to their children. Your child will see a set of 20 clue boxes, each with two comments. He or she must pick one of the two comments in each clue box based on which comment they like better. Explain that at the end of all the clues, you and your child can count the clues he or she circled and solve the mystery. If your child asks what the "mystery" is or what it is about, you can simply explain that it's a game in which parents are trying to learn what makes kids happy or what they like to hear their parents say.

To give this a game-like effect, you should secretly write on a piece of paper what you think your child's love language is (words, touch, time, service, gifts). That is, which letter will he or she most often circle? Do not let your child see your guess but tell him or her that you have written down your guess and will find out at the end of the game if you guessed right. After your child has gone through the set of clues, help him or her count and transfer the answers to the appropriate blanks. Reveal your guess and tell your child if you guessed correctly. For your knowledge, **A** = Physical Touch, **B** = Words of Affirmation, **C** = Gifts, **D** = Acts of Service, and **E** = Quality Time.

This activity will have been little more than a game to your child to see if he or she got the same answer to the "mystery" that you got. He or she will have little clue that you're using this information to further confirm or clarify your guess about his or her love language. Because children expect games to end in a "reward," tell your child at the end of the "mystery solving" that, whether or not you guys ended up with the same answer, you'll celebrate by doing something fun together (i.e., eating a favorite snack, watching a movie, playing a game of your child's choosing, etc.).

Some children will help "solve the mystery" and be satisfied not asking any questions. If your child happens to inquire about this so-called mystery you wanted help with, give a brief explanation of the love languages and tell your child that you just want to make sure he or she recognizes and receives your love. Depending on your child's maturity level, he or she may be able to share his or her thoughts on the matter and further clarify his or her love language.

You are now ready to introduce your child to "The Love Language Mystery Game." At the top of the "game" or profile, you'll see a brief set of instructions that explain to your child how to take and score the profile. Because of your child's age and potential questions he or she may have, be prepared to read the instructions to him or her and answer any questions he or she may have. Also be prepared to help your child score the profile by helping him or her count the number of times he or she circled each letter (A, B, C, D, E). Finally, if your child needs help transferring his or her scores to the appropriate blanks at the end of the profile, then offer to assist with that as well. Have fun, and enjoy unlocking the mystery of your child's love language!

THE LOVE LANGUAGES MYSTERY GAME

Each clue box has two comments that parents sometimes make to their children. Read each clue box and, of the two comments, pick the one you like better and wish your mom or dad would say to you. Then circle the letter that goes with that comment. Be careful and only circle one letter in each clue box! After you've gone through all 20 clue boxes, go back and count how many A's, B's, C's, D's, and E's that you circled. Then write your scores in the blanks at the end of the game. Ask your mom or dad for help if you have any questions. And have fun unlocking the love language mystery!

1
Give me a hug!   A
You are terrific!   B

2
I've got a special birthday present for you!   C
I'll help you with your project.   D

3
Let's go to a movie.   E
Give me a high five!   A

4
You are so smart!   B
Have you made your Christmas list?   C

5
Would you help me cook dinner?   D
I like going to fun places with you!   E

6
Give me a kiss!   A
You are #1!   B

7
I've got a surprise for you. — C
We can make something really cool. — D

8
Let's watch TV together! — E
Tag, you're it! — A

9
You did a great job! — B
You've earned a special surprise! — C

10
You can invite your friends. — D
Let's go to your favorite restaurant. — E

11
I'm going to give you a big hug! — A
You are an awesome kid! — B

12
I made your favorite food. — C
I checked your homework, and it looks great! — D

13
You are fun to hang out with! — E
I'll race you! — A

14
Wow! You did it! — B
Check under your bed for a special present! — C

15
I cleaned up your room for you. — D
Let's play a game together. — E

16
Would you like for me to scratch your back? — A
You can do it! Don't give up! — B

17
What would you like for your birthday? — C
We can pick up your friend on the way to the movie. — D

18
I always like doing stuff with you. — E
You are so huggable! — A

19 How did you know how to do that? You are brilliant!   **B**
I can't wait to give you your present!   **C**

20 Don't worry! I'll pick you up on time!   **D**
Let's spend the day doing whatever you want to do!   **E**

How many **A**'s did you circle? _____
A's stand for physical touch. People whose love language is physical touch like to receive hugs, kisses, and high fives.

How many **B**'s did you circle? _____
B's stand for words of affirmation. People whose love language is words of affirmation like for others to use words to tell them that they are special and that they do a good job.

How many **C**'s did you circle? _____
C's stand for gifts. People with the love language of gifts feel good when someone gives them a special present or surprise.

How many **D**'s did you circle? _____
D's stand for acts of service. A person whose love language is acts of service likes it when others do nice things for them such as helping with chores, helping with school projects, or driving them places.

How many **E**'s did you circle? _____
E's stand for quality time. People with the love language of quality time like it when others do things with them like watch a movie, go out to eat, or play a game.

Now ask your mom or dad what letter he or she guessed you would circle the most? Write the letter he or she guessed in this blank.

_____

Did your mom or dad guess the same letter that you chose most often when playing the love language mystery game? Circle: Yes or No

CONGRATULATIONS! You've solved the love language mystery and figured out what your love language is! Good job!

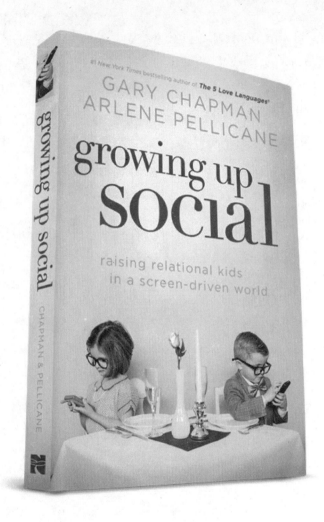